RESTAURANT MARKETING AND ADVERTISING

For Just a Few Dollars a Day

By Amy S. Jorgensen

The Food Service Professionals Guide To:
Restaurant Marketing and Advertising
For Just a Few Dollars a Day: 365 Secrets Revealed

Atlantic Publishing Group, Inc. Copyright © 2003
1210 SW 23rd Place
Ocala, Florida 34474
800-541-1336
352-622-5836 - Fax

www.atlantic-pub.com - Web Site
sales@atlantic-pub.com E-mail

SAN Number :268-1250

International Standard Book Number: 0-910627-13-4

Library of Congress Cataloging-in-Publication Data

Jorgensen, Amy S., 1975-
Restaurant marketing & advertising for just a few dollars a
day: 365 secrets revealed / by Amy S. Jorgensen.
p. cm. -- (The food service professionals guide to ; 3)
Includes bibliographical references and index.
ISBN 0-910627-13-4 (pbk. : alk. paper)
1. Hospitality industry--Marketing. 2. Advertising--
Hospitality industry.   I. Title. II. Title: Restaurant
marketing and advertising for just a few dollars a day. III.
Series.
TX911.3.M3J67 2002
647.95'068'8--dc21

2002011460

Printed in Canada

Book layout and design by Meg Buchner of Megadesign
www.mega-designs.com • e-mail: megadesn@mhtc.net

CONTENTS

*Loyal customers
are the key to
continued success.*

INTRODUCTION

Profitability is what's going to keep you in business. How and where you focus to become, and stay, profitable is the key. Are you crunching numbers and pushing your servers to raise their check averages, or are you creating an environment that leaves patrons feeling served and eager to come back? Are you holding staff meetings that leave your crew energized or deflated? Are management, kitchen and waitstaffs working independently or as a complete whole towards a common goal? This manual will give you invaluable insights into how and where you can implement internal and external marketing changes in your business. It will also tell you how you can boost your sales volume 15-50 percent in the process, with very little cost.

Marketing and advertising, as you will find out, involves every aspect of your business. All components feed into each other in an ongoing circle that includes the menu, staff training, food presentation, knowledge of patrons, advertising, promotions, customer service, distribution, research, pricing, sales, public relations, product development and packaging. No one thing is more important than another; all are essential.

Restaurant Marketing and Advertising For Just a Few Dollars a Day: 365 Secrets Revealed will give you some exciting ideas for each of the above-mentioned categories, plus it will examine a few other strategies.

Cheers!

Loyal, repeat customers can increase your volume drastically.

CHAPTER ONE

CUSTOMERS FOR LIFE

Take Care of Your Guests - And Your Sales Will Take Care of Themselves!

Customers for life means that once guests come to your restaurant, they'll never be satisfied with your competitors. It also means that the real work of building sales doesn't happen with your advertising schedule or marketing plan, but on the floor with your customers. How do you do this? The following tips could mean the difference between success and failure:

- **The key to building restaurant sales is to increase volume from your existing customer base.** Think about it: if your customers were to return just one more time per month, that would be an increase in sales volume of between 15 and 50 percent! These are people who already know about you, live within an acceptable travel distance and will recommend you to their friends if you make them happy. These are the people you want to target in order to build a regular, loyal customer base that share the pleasures of your establishment with friends.

- **Work on building loyalty**, **not the check average!** It's true: a bigger check is a bigger sale. However, selling techniques designed to boost check averages can be dangerous to the survival of your business. Your income comes from serving people, not food. Focusing only on the bottom line puts your customers second at best. If everyone who ever ate at your restaurant were so pleased that he couldn't wait to come back with his friends, what would your sales be like? If eating with you didn't thrill your customers, if they felt pressured to order something expensive, what difference does it make how big their check was when they won't be coming back?

- **This isn't to say that suggestive selling can't work.** If it's done well it can be very effective. There is an entire manual on this subject from this series. The problem is it's almost never done well and you run the risk of your guests thinking they come in a distant second to their money. The safest way to achieve sales growth is to have your guests return more often. Focusing on this is a win-win situation. Your goal is to delight them, win their loyalty and put them first! If you're a restaurant patron - and you are - what will have you coming back for another meal: your waiter focusing on getting you to spend more money or treating you like royalty?

Guest Expectations - The Specifics

Do you know what your customers expect when they come through the door? Are you out to exceed those expectations and give each guest a memorable and delightful meal every time? Here's how to establish what is expected of you:

- **Do your own SWOT.** SWOT is an acronym that stands for Strengths, Weaknesses, Opportunities and Threats. It is a great exercise to do before you begin developing your marketing strategy. Simply outline all of these areas regarding your restaurant. What is your restaurant good at? How strong is the competition you're going to be facing and from where is it coming? These are the questions you need to ask yourself. Then keep these things in mind as you develop your approach.

- **Don't delay marketing until you need it!** Marketing is not something you do when business is slow. In fact, if you wait until then, it may be too late. Studies have shown that the major marketing efforts you set in motion now won't pay off for another three to six months! In order to keep profits high and your customer base growing, marketing needs to be a daily part of your business. For further information about marketing your restaurant, see the following Web sites: www.restaurant-marketing.net and www.restaurantmarketing.com.

- **Don't rely on one method.** Let's say you decide to go crazy and develop a commercial for your restaurant. It takes every penny of your marketing budget, but you manage to produce it and get it on television. What if it isn't successful? What if it brings customers in once, but because you have nothing set in place to encourage repeat business, they never come back? You don't want to put all your effort into one medium or one type of marketing. Remember, every component of the process is equally important.

- **Don't change what works.** Maybe you are already running a monthly promotion that has doubled your lunch business. Should you abandon that just because you find another appealing idea in this manual? Absolutely not! If you have something that works for you, don't stop it. You may want to tweak it a little or incorporate some new ideas into your current promotion, but never end a marketing tool that has brought you success. It would be like eliminating the most popular item on your menu.

- **Identify your target audience.** In order to develop an effective marketing approach, you have to understand whom you want to come to your restaurant. Are you trying to attract upscale, business executives or do you want families to frequent your establishment?

- **Identify your goal.** Before you decide on your marketing approach, you must decide on a goal for your efforts. Do you want to boost your sales by $2,000 per week? Do you want to triple the number of customers coming to Happy Hour? Once you decide where you want to be, it's easier to figure out how to get there.

- **Keep a marketing notebook.** Always make sure to document your marketing efforts. Write down the promotions you are trying, keep track of your goals and make notes when you visit other restaurants.

Delight Your Guests

Satisfaction isn't even close to good enough. It's an improvement on dissatisfaction, of course, but in today's very tough market, it won't keep people coming back. There is just too much competition. You need to exceed your guests' expectations, every time. The food-service business is built on personal connections. You serve one person at a time and the more personal that interaction, the more you'll exceed their expectations - and the happier they will be. Here are some guidelines and hints for meeting basic guest expectations:

- **Guests expect the restaurant staff to care.**

- **Knowledge.** Guests expect their servers to know the menu and how dishes are prepared and to be able to answer questions about the wine list.

- **Guests expect hot food hot and cold food cold.** Serve cold food on a chilled, not frozen, plate. Try removing your heat lamps altogether; they don't keep food hot and they can cause your staff to delay in getting food to your guests.

- **Timing.** From order to delivery, guests expect their drinks within 2 minutes, appetizers in 5-10 minutes, entrées in 15-25 minutes and dessert in 3-5 minutes. Check turnaround should take no more than 2 minutes. At the beginning and end of a meal, guests are the least tolerant of delays. Make sure your staff doesn't keep people waiting after they've been seated or when they're ready to leave.

Show Your Customers that You Care

Often it is your attention to finer details that will indicate to customers that you really care. It's the surest way to convert casual diners into regular patrons. Try a few of the following tips:

- **Use unique table settings.** Regular place settings are what your guests expect, but you'll never make an extraordinary impression by just meeting their expectations. You want to exceed them. Consider using unusual plates and silver, weird glasses, or an unusual table decoration. One restaurant lets patrons paint their own martini glasses; another in New York City has a replica of the Empire State Building on the table. Near the inlet? How about a model of a lighthouse? Plates can be glass, planks of wood, rock, even banana leaves. After all, if your food is unique, your utensils should be also. Customers will pilfer some, but when they show their conquest to their friends, they will talk about your establishment. Plus, you can sell them in your little boutique store and on your Web site.

- **Use patron pagers for waiting guests.** Few restaurants have enough seating room for the guests waiting to get in on a busy Friday or Saturday night. A patron pager allows guests to journey a little farther from the building without straining to hear each muffled name. The pager (there are a multitude of varieties) automatically goes off when the seat is available. Plus, pagers lessen the chance of waiting guests becoming impatient and leaving. You can purchase these from a number of companies such as www.jtech.com, www.crstexas.com and www.mat-technologies.com.

- **ATMs.** You want to limit the number of obstacles between you and a customer as much as possible. Consider installing an ATM in the lobby for guest convenience.

- **Keep the restroom sparkling.** One of the first signs of your restaurant's dedication to customers is the cleanliness, or lack thereof, of your restroom facilities. Guests will form an impression of your establishment from their visit. Soap, paper towel and toilet tissue dispensers should be filled at all times to prevent embarrassing and unhygienic problems for guests. Also, have twice as many restrooms for women. Another tip is to provide diaper-changing materials in both the men's and women's restrooms.

- **Choose appropriate background music.** One of the biggest irritations to guests is background music that is either too loud or inappropriate. Get it right.

- **Make adjustments for patrons with disabilities.** While legally your establishment must be accessible to disabled patrons, there are no laws forcing you to welcome them. That is something you should do on your own.

- **Have menus in Braille.** Braille and picture-only menus can be created at www.brailleenterprises.com or through select vendors at www.hotbraille.com, . Make sure that guests in wheelchairs can be comfortably accommodated in your dining areas. You will also want to include some training for your staff members so they will be well prepared to deal with the special needs of these guests.

- **Provide reading materials for single diners.** When single guests come in for a meal, you can help make their experience a little more pleasant by providing free newspapers, books and magazines for their reading enjoyment. It may also be a nice way for two singles to strike up a conversation and when couples meet at your restaurant, you can be sure they'll be back many times to relive the moment.

- **Provide calculators with check.** When guests need to split the check or figure a tip, it can be annoying for them to try to figure the amounts in their head or to dig through their purses to find a calculator. The problem can easily be resolved by presenting a calculator with the check. Guests can use it and the server can pick it up along with the money. Or, provide it at no charge imprinted with your name and perhaps a tipping chart on the back.

- **Create a designated driver program.** Drunk driving is a big problem. You can do your part to protect yourself and to prevent accidents by implementing a designated driver program. When anyone buys a drink at a table, your servers should be instructed to mention the program to the guests and encourage them to participate. The details can be on a table tent they place on the table. The designated driver of the group should then receive all nonalcoholic beverages free. You have the option of limiting this to coffee, tea and colas or including "virgin" mixed drinks Make sure your program involves free taxi service as well.

- **Provide delivery service for the elderly.** Elderly diners may not always be able to leave the house in order to eat at your restaurant, no matter how much they may want to. You can keep their business by offering a delivery service for them. You may want to have a special menu of reasonably priced items available for delivery. Give a copy of the menu to elderly guests who come into the restaurant. Also, consider distributing the menu to seniors' activities clubs and churches. Go a step further and deliver a rose to the table.

- **Give turned-away customers a voucher.** When your restaurant is overcrowded and you still have guests wanting to come in for food, you may need to be honest and turn some people away. Never turn them away without giving them a reason to come back another time. Show them that their patronage is important to you. You may want to give them a voucher for a free dessert or a discount on their next visit.

- **Cater to pets.** If your restaurant has any outdoor seating, you may want to consider offering service to your guests' pets as well. Pet owners have a deep connection with their animals and think of them as family. The opportunity to take them out on an excursion will be incredibly appealing to most of them. Think Seattle and Starbucks. Make sure to provide the pets water and food and that all customers keep their dogs on a leash.

- **Guarantee everything.** It may seem crazy, but people are willing to take risks when they don't have anything to lose. A guarantee isn't so much a promise that everything is refundable anyway, it's more of a promise that you plan to deliver high-quality food and service at all times.

Offer Something Extra

While occasional visits from guests may be nice and a surge in numbers caused by a contest or promotion may help your bottom line significantly, the core of your survival is based on your repeat customer business. How do you turn those one-timers into regular patrons? You create a memorable experience and give customers a reason to come back. When you do both, you will increase the number of people who think of your restaurant first when they want to enjoy a dining experience. Here are some ways you can accomplish your goal:

- **Offer complimentary drinks/snacks while customers wait.** Most people hate waiting, so if your customers are loyal enough to wait more than 10 minutes for a table in your establishment, they deserve something extra. Consider giving them free snacks (pretzels, salsa and chips, etc.) or drinks (cola, water, etc.). Consider an outside patio waiting area with cocktail service. Use fans in the summer and heaters in the winter.

- **Offer free postcards.** Are you in an area with a lot of tourism? Give away free postcards to guests. You can either use postcards based on the attractions in your city or go one step further and create postcards depicting your restaurant. You can even offer to mail the cards for free! You can purchase tourism postcards through your local visitors' bureau, create your own with the help of Kinkos or other office supply stores or by visiting a site such as www.vistaprint.com.

- **Offer free valet service.** Parking is always a hassle for guests, but unless you're an upscale restaurant, few will be willing to pay extra for valet. Stand out and offer it free, especially on Friday and Saturday nights. Your guests will love this added luxury.

- **Offer free umbrellas during bad weather.** Sometimes rain and snow showers just come up unexpectedly and many of your patrons may not be prepared for the storm. You can do them a big service by offering free umbrellas (with or without your logo). They can then return the umbrellas on their next visit (some actually will), or they'll serve as great advertisements for your restaurant every time it rains. Either way, you'll benefit. If you do opt for umbrellas displaying your logo, you can visit www.arhpromotions.com to get pricing and ordering information or check your local Yellow Pages.

- **Offer free local phone calls.** You can also use a cell phone so that you are not tying up your business line. Most have unlimited local call plans now.

- **Offer free event cakes.** When people come to your restaurant to celebrate their birthdays, anniversaries or other special occasions, it's a compliment to you. It means that your establishment is special to them, so return the gesture by showing them how special their business is to you by providing free cakes. The cakes don't have to be large masterpieces; they can be simple yet plentiful enough for at least six guests. Keep in mind that people who celebrate also tend to bring larger parties and spend more money, so making a good impression and bringing in more special-event business is worth the small amount you'll be spending. Take it one step further and write the customer's name on the cake. Also have a cake box to take home the extras.

- **Include simple surprises with carry-out orders and "doggy bags."** When someone orders something "to go" or requests a "doggy bag," you can make a nice impression by throwing in something extra. You may want to include some extra sauce, a little garnish, some mints, a small portion of a dessert or appetizer, etc. The options are unlimited.

- **Offer free samples.** While guests wait for a seat or their meal, you can leave a lasting impression and boost sales by having a server offer them free samples of your entrees, side dishes or appetizers. The samples should simply provide a taste to give diners a sense of what is to come.

- **Include hooks for coats/purses at table.** Where to put coats and purses so they don't interfere with the dining experience has always been a problem for diners. In a booth, you end up wrinkling coats. On the back of a chair, other patrons always seem to step on them. No one wants to hang their purse or coat on a rack out of view, so solve this age-old problem by putting hooks on the tables. You can place purse hooks under the tables so they are nearby, but out of the way. Coat hooks can be placed on the outside of booths or hung on coat racks within eye range of guests. This small courtesy will make a big difference with your customers.

- **Provide imaginative after-dinner treats.** How many times have you been out to dinner only to receive the customary mint along with your check? It's fine to give out mints, but why be ordinary? Remember, the way to make a splash is to stand out. Consider giving out mini-chocolates, unusual mints, a small rose or elegant hard candy. Always be on the lookout for something different even after you start distributing one variety or another. Also, make sure to have a special after-dinner treat just for children, such as a lollipop. Print your name or place a small sticker with your restaurant's name on the item.

- **Offer something extra with gift certificates.** Around the holiday seasons, gift certificates are popular items. You can double their effectiveness and popularity by giving a little something extra to the buyer of the certificates as well. Coupons, discounts and freebies are great little bonuses for shoppers. Offer an extra $10 gift certificate with every $50 gift certificate purchased.

- **Offer dedicated meeting rooms.** If you're planning on marketing to business executives, you may want to set aside some restaurant space for dedicated meeting rooms. After all, it is hard to hold an important meeting amid the ruckus of the lunch or dinner crowd. The meeting rooms are essentially private dining areas without the romantic atmosphere. Make sure to let your target audience know the rooms are available.

Create a Loyal Patron Program (LPP)

One of the easiest ways to keep guests coming back is to develop a Loyal Patron Program (LPP). Basically, these programs reward guests for their repeat business, usually with a free meal. Pick one that will be easy to put in place and will work well with the tone of your restaurant. Consider the following options:

- **Implement a punch card program.** For example, start a Loyal Lunchtime Patron Program, then for each lunch meal (over a certain price or from a select menu) the guest receives one punch on their card. After filling the card (usually 10-12 punches), they receive a free lunch. You may also want to designate certain days as double punch days.

- **Another popular LPP is called a point-on-dollar program.** With this type of program, guests earn points based on how much they spend. You may give one point for each dollar or 10 points for each $5. Then, have reward levels for the points. Perhaps at 20 points they are eligible for a free dessert; maybe at 50 they get a free meal. The specifics depend on your prices and how you implement the program. Just keep in mind that the rewards must seem attainable. Today, a simple computer database program can track this information as well as pertinent dates, such as birthdays, anniversaries, etc.

- **Sell dinner cards.** Dinner cards can be especially popular for a lunchtime crowd. Let's say your average lunch is $9 with a drink. You can sell your lunch card for $50. Then, the buyer of the card simply shows it to the server and the lunch is deducted from the card. The card should be good for, say, seven lunches, so essentially they'll be getting one free. Since people are often reluctant to leave a tip when their meal is free, you may want to figure in a 15 percent tip into the price of the card as well.

- **Start a zealot club.** Many times customers who frequent your establishment become interested in how their delicious meals are made. Also, if you specialize in one food item (e.g., steak, fish, etc.), they may have questions about how to select and cook that item on their own. For these inquisitive customers, you may want to create a zealot club. The zealot club should include a newsletter with cooking tips and restaurant news. They should also be privy to special events, such as tasting sessions for new items or tours of the kitchen. You can make membership free or charge a small fee, but you'll be sure to continue to receive their business in the future. In order to produce the newsletter inexpensively, you may want to start out doing it yourself using a computer program, such as Microsoft Publisher. Developing the mailing list with e-mail addresses will make the entire process free.

Extra Tips for Converting Casual Customers Into Loyal Patrons

When you have guests who come in frequently, let them know you notice them and appreciate their business by sending them a handwritten thank you note. Add a "Look forward to seeing you next time" to the closing of the note and you'll be seeing the receiver walk through your door within a week. Here are some additional ways in which to develop loyal patronage:

- **Buy regular guests a bottle of wine.** When you see the same face every weekend or every other weekend, you know you have yourself a loyal customer. Say thank you for their continuing patronage by buying them a bottle of wine. Take the wine over personally, thank them for being frequent diners and wish them a great evening. The effects will be well worth the cost.

- **Create a "Wall of Fame" for regulars**. Regular customers like to feel special. Consider making a wall of your restaurant into a Wall of Fame for those diners. Take a photograph of the customer and maybe even add a short bio including their first name, favorite meal, etc. The guest will not only keep coming back, but they'll bring their friends to show off their "celebrity" status. Post the "wall" to your Web site as well.

- **Create a free-meal card.** A free-meal card is essentially a card you sell for a set price, let's say $30. The holder of that card then receives one meal free with the purchase of a meal, perhaps for 15 visits. The lower-priced meal is the one that is deducted. Because they pay out the money for the card in advance, they are more likely to come back for future visits. You can also offer special events or discounts for holders of these cards to give them an extra incentive to purchase the card and come back.

- **Use bounce back certificates.** Bounce back certificates are given to a guest for use during their next visit. The certificates can be for discounts or free drinks, desserts or appetizers. When the certificates are redeemed, you can track the success of your campaign. Plus, if you ask for customers' names and addresses on the certificates, you'll be able to use them to create a computer database of your customers.

- **Use customer referral postcards.** Instruct your servers to include one of these referral cards with each bill. The postcard should have a space for the current customer to include his or her name and other information. It should also offer a discount or promotion for the customer being referred. Explain to guests that they will receive a thank-you gift by mail for each customer they refer. To keep costs low, you may want to create your own using Microsoft Publisher or similar software or visit local office supply stores. You can also order them online at www.vistaprint.com and similar sites.

- **Reward referring customers.** For each of the customer referral postcards that are redeemed, send the customer who referred the new patrons a voucher for a free dessert, free drink, discount, etc. When they come back in to redeem the voucher, they'll receive another referral postcard and a chance for another discount. You may want to vary the rewards each time so they won't get bored.

- **Start a mug club.** Actually, this idea isn't limited to mugs; it can be adapted to countless possibilities. You just need to find one that works with your restaurant. Basically, for a fee, the patron receives a personalized mug that is kept at the bar. Every time they visit, they drink out of their special mug and receive discounts on the drinks as well. The membership is a good way to keep customers coming back. You can purchase personalized mugs at a number of online stores including www.tagdesigns.com, www.arhpromotions.com and www.myron.com.

- **Adapt the "Cracker Barrel" concept.** Cracker Barrel rents audio books for travelers. Customers pay a fee, take the tape and return it to any Cracker Barrel location. Not only does this service encourage travelers to stop there once, it gives them a reason to come back. While you may not be a nationally recognized chain yet, you can find ways to put similar programs to work for you, perhaps by loaning out cookbooks or by handing out umbrellas during bad weather.

- **Teach customers.** You will make your restaurant stand out if you provide more than just an eating experience. Consider taking the opportunity to teach customers as well. Have an exhibition kitchen, a kitchen table or tours of the cooking area. Consider walking all new customers through the kitchen first. Provide newsletters with food-related information, recipes and tips for selecting perfect ingredients. Take every opportunity to educate, as well as entertain, your guests.

CHAPTER TWO

MARKETING THE MENU

Food/Menu Marketing

Your menu is your chief marketing tool. The design and presentation send a message to your customers about your theme, atmosphere and clientele. The food selection and the frequency of item rotation will keep your diners coming back or send them packing forever. The choices available for children, vegetarians and the health-conscious will either eliminate or captivate whole demographic groups. Obviously, this powerful piece is vital to the success of your restaurant. Let's look at some suggestions you can use to make your menu a piece of marketing that works for, not against, you.

- **Develop signature appetizers.** You need to be unique in order to be successful. Create one or two appetizers that stand out among the traditional cheese sticks, chicken wings and onion blossoms. Consider matching the appetizer to your restaurant's food style or theme. Give it an original name that patrons will remember.

- **Develop signature desserts.** Wave the creativity wand over your dessert list. With desserts, sometimes it may only take an added ingredient or a special presentation to make yours one-of-a-kind. For example, offer traditional cheesecake topped with coffee-flavored crème, crumbled cookies or mangos. It's still cheesecake, but with a little something extra.

- **Offer dessert samplers.** Have you ever looked at the dessert cart and thought, I'd love to have a little bit of everything? If you have, you're not alone. Make the decision a little easier by creating a sampler using small portions of all your signature desserts. Charge a little more than you would for an ordinary dessert and always bring multiple spoons because many of your diners may opt for sharing these delicious morsels.

- **Offer appetizer samplers.** How often do diners agree on what looks good? Rarely might be an overstatement. Yet, most restaurants still force diners to choose one appetizer to appease the appetites of every member of their party. Consider creating an appetizer sampler. You can create your own sampler with specific components or allow diners to mix and match their favorites.

- **Have side dishes available.** Many restaurants create entrées that include specific side items, such as the traditional steak, baked potato and salad. But what if your customer doesn't feel like having a baked potato? Or, what if they dislike iceberg lettuce? Your goal is to satisfy the customer, not to force them to eat what you tell them. It's always a good idea to create some optional and creative side dishes. Just make sure to list them plainly on your menu along with the additional price per side item or your substitution policy.

- **Create imaginative side dishes.** Most restaurants spend all their time focused on developing outstanding entrées. But let's be honest; how much can you really do with prime rib or barbecued ribs? With side dishes, you can use a little more flair. For example, offer Smashed Garlic Potatoes as a side dish. You may not be able to enhance the natural flavor of a juicy steak, but you can accentuate it with an unusual and tasty side dish.

- **Offer vegetarian alternatives.** Once thought of as a fad, more "regular" diners are increasingly abandoning meat altogether either for their health or out of respect for animals. Some people just like something a little different, a little meatless. While adding the standard veggie burger is a start, it won't help you win any vegan converts. Consider creating a vegetarian version of a popular entree, such as fajitas or pasta or develop signature vegetarian dishes using peppers, spinach or squash as the chief ingredient instead of poultry or fish. Also consider adding vegetarian alternatives to your appetizer menus.

- **Include regional favorites.** Is there one particular item in your area that stands out as a traditional favorite? You will undoubtedly find at least one. Add it to your menu. You may want to create it "as is" or add your own little flair to it, but either way it will help you stand out as a restaurant that knows the tastes of its community.

- **Offer free seconds and refills.** This concept will definitely set you apart from the crowd. Obviously, this idea won't work with all restaurants, but if you specialize in traditional home-cooking or pasta - think Olive Garden's Unlimited Pasta & Salad Bowls & Breadsticks - this could be perfect for your establishment. Most patrons won't ask for seconds, but they all appreciate having the option.

- **Allow substitutions.** What seems like a perfect pairing to some may sound very unappetizing to others. Allow guests the freedom to substitute other side items without additional cost.

- **Offer warm, interesting, "signature" fresh bread.** Many restaurants stick with the old reliable dinner rolls or biscuits to accentuate their offerings. Consider making your bread a signature item by cooking up individual loaves of pumpernickel or rye or bringing in baskets of muffins, honey-flavored rolls and more.

- **Use a unique butter.** Now that you have your interesting bread, what are you going to give patrons to top it? If you've taken the time to create a wonderful bread product, take a few minutes more to come up with a delicious butter as well. Honeys, spices and herbs are popular flavors you can add to traditional butter to make it fabulous; try your own unique combinations. Get customers talking!

- **Have the chef deliver the food, occasionally.** Don't forget to let your chef out of the kitchen every now and then. Having the chef bring out the food personally often impresses guests. It makes customers feel important, plus it allows the chef to see the pleasure his or her hard work brings to the diners.

Beverage/Menu Marketing

Here are some winning tips for marketing your beverages:

- **Develop signature drinks:** You want to be unique to get customers talking about your establishment, so develop a couple of signature drinks at your restaurant. Be as creative as possible, but try to match the drink's flavor with your restaurant's atmosphere. Make it colorful, use creative garnishes and make it fun.

- **Integrate a wine/alcohol list into the menu.** Spell out your wine suggestions in the body of the menu. You'll notice that a lot of patrons will gladly take your advice.

- **Offer nonalcoholic alternatives.** The average mixed drink costs around $4-$6, while a cola or tea runs about $1-$2, so which beverages would you rather sell the most of? Not everyone can drink alcohol. Some are designated drivers, some are recovering alcoholics, others are underage and still more just prefer to stay away from alcohol. Move them out of the cola line by offering and advertising more nonalcoholic alternatives. The easiest approach is to offer alcohol-free versions of your signature drinks and other specialties, such as mudslides and daiquiris. Also, consider creating some brand new ones.

- **Provide free refills on soft drinks.** Most restaurants offer free refills of coffee and iced tea, but patrons will also respond positively to offers for free soft drink refills. Offering free refills forces your service staff to be more attentive to each table because they need to keep the glasses full.

- **Stock only quality brands in your bar.** You want patrons to perceive your restaurant as a quality establishment so don't ruin it by serving cheap alcohol. When you stock your bar's shelves, make sure you include only top brands, such as Absolut, Jack Daniel's, Heineken, etc. When diners see brands they recognize and respect, they're more likely to transfer those positive feelings to you.

Menu Presentation

Not only must your menu look attractive, it must also provide guests with exactly what they want. Here are some suggestions for getting that balance right:

- **Use a separate menu for desserts, appetizers, wine, nonalcoholic beverages, etc.** Very few people order their entire meal from drink to dessert at one time, yet most restaurants combine the menus for all of these items into one and take it away once patrons order their entrées. Without descriptions of gooey desserts and luscious mixed drinks at their fingertips, diners will most likely pass on those items. Create small menus for these various articles including detailed descriptions and vivid pictures. Keep them on the table so guests will be able to peruse them as they wait and you'll see a dramatic increase in sales. Have a menu program, such as Menu Pro from www.atlantic-pub.com to develop your menus – and save a bundle in design and printing fees.

- **Develop a story for your menu.** People love a place that has a little history, even a fictional one.

Consider turning the story of your restaurant (or an embellished account) into part of your menu. It gives diners something to read and discuss while they are waiting for their servers or food. You can also use your "story" to market other items, such as cookbooks and T-shirts.

- **Use special icons for signature items.** If you design signature entrées, desserts, drinks or appetizers, let your patrons know it. Create a special icon - a star, your logo or a representation of your restaurant - and place it beside all of your signature items. The icon will attract patrons' attention, especially if they arc looking to try something new and inventive.

- **Create a separate section for healthy foods.** While it is an excellent idea to add some healthy menu options, avoid labeling them with icons. Studies have shown these icons actually hurt the sales of an item, possibly because a low-fat entrée rarely sounds as tasty when it's above a succulent description of high-fat red beef. Instead, make a separate section on your menu for all of your healthier choices. By doing this, you minimize competition from the tempting, but unhealthy, fare. For some healthy food menu ideas and recipes, visit the Web site www.foodfit.com.

- **Incorporate brand names into name or description of item.** Have you been to T.G.I. Friday's? If so, you are probably familiar with their Jack Daniel's line of entrees. These meals are a perfect example of this suggestion. Many of your entrées, appetizers and even desserts probably rely on name-brand ingredients. Let the diners know by incorporating those brands into either your item's name or at least into its description. The reputation of the product will help boost sales of those items.

- **"A picture is worth a thousand words."** People eat with all of their senses, especially their eyes, so if you can show them how tasty your items are, you have them sold. Make sure that the photo accurately portrays the item. Nothing is more disappointing to a customer than receiving a meal that does not look like its picture.

- **Keep negative statements off menu.** Have you been to a restaurant where the menu says "No checks accepted" or "We reserve the right to refuse service to anyone"? Negatively phrased comments or rules send a negative impression of you to your patrons. Instead, simply include what you do accept: cash, all credit cards, etc. Get the point across without the negativity.

- **Give clever names to food items.** When is a hamburger just a hamburger? When you don't want to sell many of them. Face it, people don't go to restaurants to eat things they can make at home, such as spaghetti, meatloaf or tossed salad. National chains know this, hence the reason all of their items that have unique names, such as Burger King's "The Whopper," and Red Lobster's "Ultimate Feast" or "RockZilla." With the right name, even the most mundane meal will seem extraordinary.

- **Name a menu item after a customer.** Having trouble thinking up interesting names for your items? Or, maybe you're looking for a way to reward loyal patronage. Either way, all you need to do is name an item after a customer. Mention on the menu that the item was named for a loyal customer. You'll have a customer who will bring in all of his or her friends, co-workers and relatives to try the eponymous-named concoction, plus you'll see an increase in loyal patrons hoping to get their own menu item as well.

Menu Adaptations

Your menu should never be cast in stone. It's important to review your menu on a regular basis. Be flexible and ready to adapt. Here are some suggestions:

- **Update regularly.** Even the most loyal patrons want to try something new. In order to stay on top, you need to update your menu regularly. You'll want to eliminate or reinvent less popular items, add a few new ones and possibly adjust your prices. However, updating too frequently may irritate customers who never get an opportunity to develop a favorite because of the changes. Twice a year is probably a good estimate. If you need to make changes or additions before then, you can always use a supplemental menu.

- **Track popularity of food items.** In order to update your menu effectively, you'll need to track the popularity of your menu items. If you use a computer or POS system to enter orders, it will do this for you. Otherwise, you will need a manual system.

- **Value.** When you're planning your menu, always keep in mind that it's not the price patrons are most concerned about, it's the perceived value.

They're willing to pay more when they get more. Make sure the "value" of your items is obvious in the descriptions and pictures on your menu and keep that "value" in line with your price.

- **Make nutritional information available.** Because people are becoming more health-conscious, they like to be informed about the food they eat. While the menu is not the appropriate place to list the nutritional information about that chocolate cake you offer, it is the best place to let diners know how they can find that information. You may want to create a small brochure or add a page to your Web site that details the fat content, calories, etc. You may also want to make this information available to weight loss programs in your area, such as Weight Watchers and Jenny Craig outlets. Software such as Chef Tec & Nutracoster, available at www.atlantic-publishing.com, will break down the nutritional information from your recipes.

- **Consider cultural trends.** Part of running a successful restaurant, or business in general, is staying on top of current trends. For example, the increase in the number of children going out to eat with their parents is a cultural trend that impacts your business, as is the growing number of vegetarians. Recognizing these trends will allow you to change your restaurant to accommodate them. The NRA publishes a great report on restaurant trends at www.restaurant.org.

- **Create an ethnic menu.** As the population continues to grow more diverse, people are more willing than ever to try items that may not be considered a standard part of their cultural appetite. Even if you serve more traditional fare, you may want to consider creating a menu with more variety. You may want to include Indian, Japanese, Mexican and Italian. Be sure to add a detailed description that includes the ingredients and possibly a picture. People are more likely to be adventurous when they can see what they will be eating. A great area to start to introduce ethnic foods is on the appetizer menu. For information about ethnic food and drink, visit *Menu Magazine* online at www.menumagazine.co.uk.

- **Create a holiday menu.** When Christmas, Thanksgiving, Easter, the Fourth of July and other holidays roll around, people begin to crave particular kinds of food: turkey, ham, deviled eggs, etc. Why not appeal to those cravings while creating a festive mood in your establishment by developing special holiday menus? You could make the menu red, white and blue to celebrate Independence Day or add a dish made with red and green tortilla chips in honor of Christmas.

- **Reinvent less popular menu items.** There are probably one or two items on your menu that just don't seem to be pulling in their share of the sales. That's no reason to drop them completely. Instead, reinvent them. Consider adding a new ingredient, changing the presentation or making it a featured selection. Make sure that the picture or description of the item is accurate. You may want to change the side dishes as well.

- **Create supplemental menus.** If you offer specials or seasonal dishes, you may want to consider creating supplemental menus. These are usually just single sheets that can be added into your traditional menu. They are ideal to advertise items that may not be staples on your menu. They are also ideal for advertising new dishes so you can test them out before revamping all of your menus.

- **Develop a late-night menu.** After a late movie, theater or an evening of dancing, the restaurant choices are limited. You could get a piece of that business simply by developing a late-night menu. Instead of offering entrees, stick to appetizers, desserts and sandwiches. Offer specialty coffees, teas, desserts and coffee drinks. Become the after-hours spot to unwind after a Friday or Saturday night of partying.

- **Feature menu items.** One of the easiest ways to boost sales of an item is to make it a featured item. Even if it has been on the menu for years, many regular patrons may never have noticed it (especially those with favorite meals), and many new customers who aren't sure what to try will trust your guidance. Before selecting a featured item, make sure that the quality, taste and presentation of the item are top-notch.

- **Create meal or value packs.** Consider packaging an appetizer, entrée and dessert for one price. You could also consider making a meal pack for two, which would be perfect for Valentine's Day or anniversaries. You could even make it special by adding champagne or wine to the package.

- **Develop all-inclusive pricing**. Many people, especially families and senior citizens, want to know how much they are spending on a meal with no surprises, which is why both groups adore all-you-can-eat buffets and fast food value meals. You can incorporate that same idea into your restaurant as

well. For example, maybe you want to offer some
lunch specials that include a sandwich, side item
and drink all for one price. You can do the same for
evening entrées.

Menu Service Options

Always be on the lookout for innovative ways to
enhance your service options. Customer preferences
are constantly shifting and it is up to you to identify
their needs. You may wish to test the market in a few of
the following areas:

- **Consider adding a low-cost "Early Bird" menu.**
  Consider adding an "Early Bird" menu with
  restricted hours for retirees or those on a
  restrictive budget. "Early Bird" hours are generally
  from 4:00 p.m. to 5:30 p.m. There are some establishments in retiree areas such as Florida and
  Arizona that do most of their business during this
  time period.

- **Offer a takeout menu.** Sometimes customers,
  especially during busy times, like to call in an
  order and pick it up with no hassle, no fuss and
  no wait. Since not all of your menu items will be
  easy to provide for takeout, you will want to create
  a special, smaller version of your menu just for
  this purpose. Include prices and phone and fax
  numbers with an order form on the menu.
  Consider a special parking space for takeout
  orders, maybe even a drive thru. Offer convenience
  to pick up the order. Cater to this growing market;
  make it a part of your business, not an inconven-
  ience.

- **Use a kiosk food cart.** Want to reach a new area of customers? Consider using a kiosk food cart. Place the cart in malls, shopping centers or business areas and sell a scaled-down menu to passers-by. Make sure that you also use the cart to advertise your main restaurant by passing out menus.

- **Offer 24-hour service.** You can set yourself apart easily by offering 24-hour service. After all, many people, including late-night workers, travelers and college students, would enjoy having a restaurant available to get a bite to eat and drink a cup of coffee. Many 24-hour restaurants offer both breakfast and lunch options to their late-night patrons while others opt for a scaled-down late-night menu only. Just make sure that the food and service are as good at 2 a.m. as they are at 2 p.m.

- **Offer Sunday brunch.** Many families still enjoy the idea of a nice Sunday meal; they just don't have the time or the energy to make it. Couples also enjoy a romantic Sunday brunch. Many brunches are provided in a buffet format so the stress on your service staff and labor costs is minimal.

- **Offer a salad bar.** A salad bar is a great idea for almost every type of restaurant. Not only will it help you appeal to vegetarians and health-conscious patrons, you will also find it to be a popular lunch option and a well-received extra to any entrée. With a salad bar, you can also offer a number of options: all-you-can-eat, one-trip or to go. The "to go" options are often priced by the ounce. The more options available, the happier your customers will be.

- **Create a packaged version of your food.** Increase sales of your food without increasing your dining capacity by selling pre-packaged versions of your entrées, appetizers and desserts. You could sell the items on your Web site, in your restaurant, even in local supermarkets. Not only will it increase your overall sales, it will reach a new audience who may never have tried your establishment.

- **Offer a buffet.** Even if you don't want to join the all-you-can-eat market, you may want to consider offering a buffet, especially on a traditionally slow evening such as Monday or Tuesday or every weekday during lunch. Desserts are generally not included. Keep drink purchases separate.

*Your success
depends on
your staff.*

CHAPTER THREE

YOUR STAFF IS YOUR BEST ASSET

Hiring

Hire employees who like people. When you make hiring decisions, you want to bring in people who are enthusiastic, bubbly and fun. You want people who love people, who want to be social butterflies. These are the people with the potential to bring you success. Here are a few important considerations when hiring staff:

- **Remember, some skills cannot be taught.** You can teach someone how to take an order, pour water without spilling it and repeat the daily specials, but you cannot teach someone how to smile, be genuine or make customers feel relaxed. These are skills that are inherent, which come from a candidate's personality, not training. Be careful about focusing too much on experience and not enough on essential interpersonal skills.

- **Hire great bartenders.** If you step into the bar of your establishment and see your patrons smiling, laughing and having a good time, you know two things: It's because of your bartender and he or she is making you a lot of money. A great bartender is chatty and welcoming. Great bartenders know how to make a good drink fantastic and they remember their regulars' favorites. People will select your restaurant just because they don't want to disappoint your amazing bartender.

- **Hire an amazing host or hostess.** The host or hostess is more than just a greeter and seater. They welcome the guests, give them a menu and show them to their seat, setting the mood for the entire evening. Great hosts and hostesses are rare finds that can start the dining experience off on the perfect foot by taking initiative (getting drink orders, bringing water, etc.) and anticipating customers' needs (bringing booster seats, giving extra napkins, etc.). They literally seem thrilled to see each customer. They also make sure that the appropriate server is on the ball about getting to the table.

- **Use undergraduates more effectively.** In many restaurants, college students make up a large proportion of the serving staff, but in many cases this is a great waste of their potential. Many of these students are majoring in fields that could be beneficial to you, especially marketing, sales, public relations, computers, etc. Find out if they may be able to assist your restaurant with other functions. It will be a great learning experience for them, plus you'll benefit from their youthful input. Their services will also cost you less than a seasoned professional. Ask your staff and/or contact the job placement department of your local colleges and universities to see if they can assist you in finding these qualified students.

Your Staff Determines the Success of Your Restaurant

Your employees are the ones who delight your guests – or don't. They give them things to talk about and provide the crucial personal connection. Staff will execute most of your sales promotions and programs, educate your customers about what makes your restaurant better than the one down the street and give your guests information they can pass on to their friends. Make the most of your staff in the following ways:

- **It's in your waitstaff's best interests to connect with customers.** After all, it's through that connection that their tip averages will go up. But, and here's the thing, your staff will treat your guests the same way that you treat your staff. If you want your staff to be gracious, to listen and delight your guests, you've got to do the same for them.

- **Staff encouragement.** If you take the pressure off your staff to get the check averages up and instead encourage them to treat their customers in a way that will bring them in one more time per month, then your waitstaff can increase their incomes in tips by as much as 50 percent! This is just through being nice and committed to serving your patrons' needs. Also, guests who know their waitpersons usually leave higher tips. As your waitstaff get to know their customers, they're not just increasing the possibility of greater revenue through repeat business, they're also increasing the chance that they'll get a bigger tip this time just by making a personal connection.

- **The waitstaff is also your primary sales force.** Your servers can determine whether someone orders an appetizer, shares a dessert or just asks for the bill. The service your guests receive is not only the concern of your serving staff, it's also vital to your host or hostess, your chef, the management, your bartender and, yes, even you!

Training Your Staff to Sell

Never underestimate the difference that training can make to the success of your establishment - not only in terms of efficiency, but also in achieving staff loyalty and commitment. Here are some useful training tips:

- **Don't encourage servers to use pre-formatted script.** "I'm Bob and I'll be your server tonight. What can I get you to drink?" How many times have you heard this from a server? What about something like this: "Hi! I'm Bob! Is this your first visit? Let me recommend our scrumptious strawberry margarita." You see the difference. A script is good for training because it gives staff members an idea of what they need to convey, but to be successful on the floor, they need to be themselves, not a robot with a great memory. For information about training waitstaff, go to www.waiter-training.com and www.restaurant.org/nfsem/keep_it_clean/train.htm.

- **Include tasting sessions.** Include at least one, possibly more, tasting sessions. Servers need to know what they're selling. This allows your staff to develop their own favorites on your menu so when someone asks what they recommend, they can sound genuinely convincing.

- **Train staff in selecting, opening and serving wine.** If your restaurant serves wine, it should be an essential part of your staff's training. Encourage your staff to view Web sites such as www.demystifying-wine.com and www.grape-varieties.com. As in food sampling, you will want to hold wine-tasting meetings.

- **Train staff to "sell" appetizers.** Which of these is more effective: "Would you like an appetizer this evening?" or "Can I bring you a delicious fresh shrimp cocktail, or possibly one of our homemade soups? I highly recommend the New England clam chowder. It is fantastic! Made fresh every day by our chef with local little neck clams." What if, after the customer hesitates a moment, the server offers to get them a free sample to try? If your appetizer is as delicious as promised, you will have won them over. The art of selling is simply not giving the customer a chance to say "no." Make sure every member of your staff masters that art.

- **Record servers during training.** Videotape a staff training session. Then, go over it with them and point out the exact areas where they can improve. They will learn better by seeing the error and learning how to correct it. Plus, if they do a good job, it will give them more confidence which will show in their performance.

- **Allow employees to assess themselves.** The videotape of their training performance can also be used to allow employees to assess themselves. Servers may make mistakes of which they are unaware. By giving them a chance to view the videotape, you give them a chance to rate their performance and make mental notes of areas on which to improve.

- **Allow employees to assess each other.** Just as students tend to learn a great deal from their peers, trainees can learn a lot from their fellow employees. Offer suggestions on dealing with a difficult situation or provide tips on taking orders more efficiently. By examining the tapes together, they can offer valuable feedback that will help new members of the staff learn and improve.

- **Invite customers to training sessions.** To give trainees a real sense of reality, consider inviting customers to one of your training sessions.

Keep Staff Informed

Have a 5-10 minute pre-shift meeting daily. Every day, gather the staff together before their shift starts and update them on specials, advertisements, featured items and drink deals. Include words of encouragement and some tips for improvement. Encourage the staff to ask questions. Remember, the meeting should be brief. An effective staff meeting is not just a gathering of bodies with one person giving out information; it's primarily a meeting that generates positive feeling in the entire group. This may be a good time to let servers taste today's specials and have the kitchen staff tell the waitstaff about them. Also, waitstaff are getting paid for this time, but not tipped, so be sure not to take advantage of their time. An effective staff meeting has three main goals:

- **Generating a positive group feeling.** This will help your staff discover what they have in common and think in terms of working together, as opposed to strictly as individuals. Share good news in order to build good feeling. Staff meetings are not a good time to address individual or group shortcomings. Find the positive (even if you need to hunt for it) and talk about it. This is how you will build a supportive feeling and get people talking.

- **Starting a dialogue.** A good dialogue is a comfortable back-and-forth of ideas that gets people connected and leaves your staff feeling that they're a truly creative part of your restaurant. You learn from the staff and they learn from you. Allowing this flow of ideas reduces or eliminates the "Us vs. Them" mentality in your staff and puts everybody on the same team. If everybody is on the same team, service improves and productivity and profits increase.

- **Training.** This is your chance not only to pass along tips to your staff, but also to have them learn from each other. Your staff are intelligent people and they instinctively know what works. Encouraging them to share thoughts about work will turn staff meetings into a forum for discussing ideas. This atmosphere will increase their learning curve dramatically.

Extra Tips for Making the Most of Your Staff

Your staff is motivated, well-informed and eager to please your guests, but there is always room for improvement. Compliment staff whenever the opportunity presents itself. Everyone likes to know that he or she is doing a good job. When you receive compliments from the guests or when you see one of your staff members doing a great job, make sure to let them know. It will boost their spirits and let them know that you are paying attention to what they are doing. To follow are some additional ways in which you can motivate your staff to market and advertise your restaurant.

- **Give business cards to all staff members.** A business card is not just a way for employees to promote themselves; it's a way to promote you as well. Servers can use their cards to encourage guests to request them upon repeat visits. Chefs can use their cards to advertise where they work. Managers will use their cards at almost every available opportunity. Business cards help get your name out into the public, plus they give people something more tangible than their memories to hold onto. Business cards can be ordered at any office supply store or through online sites, such as www.vistaprint.com.

- **Keep employees informed of specials/ advertisements.** Have a regular meeting to announce upcoming specials and advertisements, then keep copies of all of them posted in the staff area so if they do have a question, they won't have to look far for an answer.

- **Advertise products with employee buttons.** When customers are trying to decide what to order, they are always looking for clues. Buttons allow just that. The buttons should mention one of your products. Make sure the product you pick has a catchy name that will stick with the customer so they won't forget what they were interested in when they look through the menu or place their order. Go online to a site such as www.1-800-my-buttons.com to place your order.

- **Select uniforms carefully.** Uniforms are important. They help guests differentiate between servers and hosts/hostesses and servers and guests, and can add to the "branding of your restaurant."

- **Keep staff informed of alcohol selections.** No server should have to ask the bartender about what drinks or alcohol is available. They should know what types of wine, beer and mixed drinks are served so when guests ask, they can give them an immediate response.

- **Start employee-incentive program.** Employees, like guests, want to feel special and recognized. Consider starting an employee-incentive program. You may want to keep track of compliments or call parties received by staff members. Either way, you should have some way of rewarding them for doing a great job. Good reward ideas might include gift certificates, a day off with pay, a small cash bonus, employee-of-the-month programs, a special employee parking space, etc.

- **Encourage staff to take initiative.** Many managers or owners try to keep their staff from making any decisions on their own regarding how best to serve the customers. Instead, staff members should be encouraged to take the lead and solve the problem, if possible, themselves.

- **Pay attention to staff perceptions.** Do your employees like their job? Do they view you as a good boss? These questions are important. How your staff perceives their position, you and the restaurant determines how they treat the customers. Unhappy workers cannot deliver outstanding service. Satisfied staff members are better salespeople, better servers, better chefs and are easier to work with overall. Conduct a survey or focus group, ask for suggestions and implement them. You'll boost morale by showing you care about their opinion.

- **Allow chefs to take risks.** Allow your chefs some creative freedom with nightly specials. Let them come up with something new to add to the menu or allow them to make suggestions for improving other items. Always remember to have a tasting session before adding any new items or changing your menu. However, you should be the one to set menu prices.

- **Allow greeters to take initial orders.** When your restaurant is busy, it may take a few minutes for your servers to get to recently seated guests just to take their drink orders. In the meantime, your guests are becoming fidgety and anxious. Instead, let the host or hostess who seats them take their initial order for drinks, water and even an appetizer. They can also explain the specials.

- **Allow time for managers to mingle with guests.** Many managers end up juggling so many responsibilities that they end up stuck in the office. Managers need to mingle and find out exactly how their staff is doing. It also enables them to handle complaints and problems more promptly.

Encourage Servers to Anticipate Customers' Needs

A good server always has his or her eye on the tables watching for possible needs. Well-trained servers seem to know instinctively when guests need drink refills or more bread sticks. This should be the goal of your other staff as well. Plus, they think ahead by bringing extra napkins to tables with children or making sure ashtrays are on tables in the smoking sections as soon as guests are seated. Servers who anticipate the needs of customers help you develop a loyal patronage.

Here are a few tried-and-tested tips:

- **Remember importance of eye contact.** Eye contact is the first and primary method of recognition your servers can employ. When they look directly at a customer and smile, they are welcoming them and making them feel comfortable. A server who does not make eye contact is either nervous or insecure, both of which make the customer feel ill at ease. Eye contact should never last more than a few seconds. Any longer and the person will become uncomfortable.

- **Say good night to exiting customers.** Good service is good from start to finish and it's not finished until the guest leaves the restaurant. Too many servers return with the change and disappear. A good server will stop, before their guests leave, to wish them a good evening and encourage them to return. Even if things were shaky in the beginning, a sincere closing can erase any negativity lingering in the customers' mind.

- **Use different-colored mugs/glasses for beverages.** It helps servers anticipate guests' needs.

- **Ensure a smooth traffic flow to buffet/salad bar.** Nothing irritates customers more at a buffet or salad bar than not knowing which way the line is moving. Your servers can help by explaining to guests where the buffet starts. Of course, you can also do your part with arrows or by placing the plates only at one end of the line.

- **Keep ashtrays on tables in smoking areas.** If a

person asks to be seated in smoking, he or she expects to be able to smoke without having to wait for a server to supply an ashtray. The longer they have to wait, the less likely they are to return.

- **Keep items on buffet/salad bar full and fresh.** Keep your buffet and salad bar full and fresh at all times. Customers will resent being kept waiting while "gaps" are being filled and your servers' "attentiveness" rating will plummet!

- **Place a dessert cart near the entrance.** Most customers aren't thinking about dessert when they enter your restaurant, so it's up to you to put it in their mind by placing a display of your most exquisite desserts near the entrance. Then, once the meal is over, bring the cart around to the table to refresh their memory.

- **Bring water to everyone at the table.** While it used to be common practice to bring water to everyone at the table, it just isn't done much anymore. However, if someone is drinking coffee or alcohol, water should certainly be provided.

- **Use personal coffee carafes.** People who drink coffee with their meals don't usually stop at one cup. Make things easier on your server by using personal coffee carafes with enough coffee for two to three cups.

- **Ask "What dessert can I bring you?"** Just as with the appetizers, you don't want your servers to give customers an opportunity to say "no." Many servers ask, "Can I get you a dessert tonight?" when they should be asking, "What dessert can I bring you?"

CHAPTER FOUR

THE COMPETITION–
STAY ONE STEP AHEAD

Evaluate Your Restaurant's Performance

Take an objective look at how well your establishment is doing. Consider the following options for evaluating your performance:

- **Use mystery shoppers.** If you want to make sure your customers are getting the highest-quality service, you may want to use a mystery shopper. Essentially, these individuals come into your restaurant like any other customer. The difference is that they report back to you every detail of their experience, both positive and negative. You can avoid the expense of involving a third-party simply by placing an ad in the newspaper yourself. Another possible way to find mystery shoppers is to approach local business colleges in your area. Many of them either teach courses on customer service or incorporate this subject into many of their classes.

- **Conduct telephone/e-mail surveys.** If you have your customers' telephone numbers or e-mail addresses (from comment cards, contest entries or reservations), you can use that valuable information to evaluate the service they received. Give them a call or send them a message. Politely introduce yourself and ask them if they have a moment to answer some questions about their last visit. Most will be happy to provide their feedback. If they seem reluctant, ask if you can send them a brief questionnaire along with a coupon for a free dessert.

- **Send employees to sample competition.** Researching your competition is essential to your restaurant's success, but it may be difficult for you to get a hands-on experience if you go there yourself. Instead, send your employees. You will get a full report on the service, food, promotions, crowd size and more.

- **Introduce a suggestion box.** Many places use a suggestion box, but few of the suggestions are ever taken. Don't let that happen. When customers make a suggestion, ask them to include their name and phone number. Then, when you check the contents of the box every week, give the customers a call and talk to them about their experiences. You'll probably find that they have many more suggestions as well. Not only will you find ways to make your establishment better, but you will also give your customers the impression that you really do care about their feedback and their opinions.

Provide Hospitality - Not Just Service

One of the best ways to stay ahead of the competition is to provide hospitality, not just service. What's the difference? Hospitality involves making a personal connection with your guests, including remembering their preferences, recognizing them as individuals and anticipating their needs. Service is simply taking their order, bringing them food and taking their money.

Hospitality keeps guests coming back; service keeps them going somewhere else. The following tips will point you in the right direction:

- **Keep track of repeat customers' usual favorites.** With regular customers, you need to stay on top of their favorites. Many will order the same thing every time they visit. Here's an example of good service: A friend of mine went to Cooker's every two weeks. She usually sat in the bar because the bartender knew her well and he always made her a Zima with grenadine. When the management of the restaurant wanted to stop selling Zima, the bartender stepped in and explained that several of their patrons regularly purchased it. That shows just one of the reasons why knowing what your customers order can make a big difference.

- **Refrain from being too chatty with guests.** While there's nothing wrong with a server making small talk with the guests (actually it should be encouraged), the server has to be able to draw the line between a chat and being chatty. Occasionally, a server may spend a little more time with a customer they know well, but only before the food is served. Once customers are engaged in eating, the server should appear only to check for additional needs, not to strike up a new conversation.

- **Remember guests' preferences.** One thing that always impresses guests is a server who remembers their preferences from visit to visit. Imagine being seated and having your server bring you your regular beverage without even having to ask what you want. That's the type of service guests remember.

- **Think of guests as family and close friends.** You know their likes and dislikes when they visit your home. You know John smokes and Susan only likes Coors Light beer from a bottle served ice cold. Bob doesn't like mushrooms or green peppers and Martha always asks for a sweater because she is often cold, even when it is not. The restaurant business is based on such hospitality.

- **Individual record cards.** You may wish to keep small note cards about regular guests' preferences. The cards could hold information about customers' likes and dislikes patterns and desires; all the information necessary to treat them like royalty. You could even reward your servers for adding to the cards each time a guest dines. Throughout this process it's VERY important never to pry; respect your customers' privacy. If a customer were reticent to share information about his life, a savvy server would note on the biography card not to ask too many questions. In this case, you're serving your customer's preferences simply by leaving him alone. Either way, you're finding out what your guests want and giving it to them.

How to Handle Complaints Better Than the Competition

Let's face it, from time to time every restaurant, however efficient, has to deal with complaints. But, all is not lost if you seize the opportunity to turn negative into positive. Handle the situation well and you'll have the guests "eating out of your hands"! Here's how it's done:

- **Provide refunds before guests request them.** If guests complain about the meal, don't wait for them to ask for their money back, offer it to them or remove the item and make an immediate substitution. When you take the initiative you are proving that you value their satisfaction. When they recount the story to their friends, they will point out how quick you were to handle the situation.

- **Resolve customer complaints in their favor.** When customers complain about their food, service, wait, etc., you should always try to resolve the issue in their favor, whether that means offering a complimentary meal, replacement and/or an apology. Customers retain favorable memories of restaurants that are proactive in rectifying their complaints.

- **Handle complaints promptly.** Whether a guest complains in person, on the phone or in writing, you cannot afford to delay your response. Take immediate action and resolve the situation. The longer you wait, the angrier the unhappy customer will become – and an angry customer is also a talkative one. If you need time to consider the situation, be honest and give them a specific deadline for your decision, then stick to it.

Discounts

Use discounts sparingly. This rule is very important. While challenging the competition, overuse of discounts will unfortunately also weaken your overall pricing structure. For example, if you consistently serve a chicken sandwich for $3 with a coupon, don't be surprised if people balk at the idea of paying $6 when it is the regular price. Used sparingly and cleverly, discounts can boost business and help you keep one step ahead of the competition, but when relied upon as your sole source of marketing, you will see an overall decline in profits. You may wish to investigate the following tried-and-tested discount possibilities:

- **Create coupons.** While coupons used to be a marketing tool employed mainly by fast food restaurants to lure in those looking for a good deal, they are now being used by almost every food chain, even popular eateries like T.G.I. Friday's and Olive Garden. The possibilities for coupons are extensive. You can offer $5 off the total check or give one meal for a reduced price with the purchase of another. You can also use coupons for free appetizers and desserts. With coupons, your objective is to bring in new customers, so make sure to include tempting pictures of your most scrumptious entrées with the coupons. You can choose to create your own or hire a printer in your area (check your local Yellow Pages or visit an office supply store).

- **Offer discounts to special groups.** Providing discounts to different groups is a good way to entice a specific audience to try your restaurant. You may want to provide discounts to students, senior citizens or even more diverse groups, such as labor unions (great idea if you are in a manu-facturing area), teachers, members of certain clubs, etc. You can either offer the discount on special days of the week, at special times or all the time.

- **Offer discounts during special times.** If you're trying to boost sales during the week or at lunch time, one way is to offer special discounts during those periods. Whether you choose to have one meal as a special or you offer a percentage discount on all tickets for a couple of hours, the discount will urge those who don't usually consider eating out at those times to give it a try.

- **Distribute mysterious envelope discounts.** You can add a bit of excitement to your discount strategy as well as increase your return business by using the mystery-envelope approach. When the server brings the check, he or she also brings a sealed envelope. Inside the envelope is a coupon or voucher good for the next visit. You may choose to include percentage discounts, lottery tickets, free desserts, etc. Either way, the guests will enjoy the surprise and will be happy to come back next time to use their discount.

- **Track coupons and gift certificates.** If you do decide to use coupons and or gift certificates, make sure you track them. Tracking them means you know which ones are redeemed, how long it takes for them to bring people in, how much people spend when they use the coupons, etc. By tracking this information, you'll be able to eliminate those coupons that aren't working, eliminate fraud and determine the overall success of your campaign. Software for tracking restaurant gift certificates may be found at www.atlantic-pub.com.

- **Use bounce backs.** Bounce backs are a great idea. These certificates, usually for discounts or free items, are received by customers at the time of their visit but are redeemable only for future visits. Generally, people have a hard time passing up a good deal, so if you give them a good time during their first visit, they'll likely return with their bounce back certificates. You don't have to continue to give out the certificates indefinitely, however. Once you have them come two or three times, chances are they'll become regulars.

- **Accept competitors' coupons.** Printing coupons can be expensive, so an inexpensive, and perhaps sneakier, option is to accept your competitors' coupons. Not only will you be able to steal customers away from surrounding restaurants, but you'll also receive all of the benefits of your own coupon campaign without the expense. You can also use this idea for research before you run your own campaign; you can identify which types of coupons typically are redeemed most frequently.

- **Give away free drinks at unusual times.** The clock says 5:46 p.m., so what does it mean? It means free drinks for everyone in the bar! Hosting a free drink giveaway at an unusual time gives customers a good reason to come in; they want something for nothing. While they wait for the freebie, they aren't going to be sitting there drinking nothing. Make sure to vary the time every day so people won't be able to plan to come in, get a free drink and go home.

- **Discounts with ticket stubs.** Since dining out and seeing movies seem to go hand in hand, why not make the most of the trend and partner with your local cinema? Offer their customers either a discount or something free when they show their ticket stubs from the cinema. To make this deal appealing to the cinema, agree to do a little promotion for them as well, perhaps by making the daily movie listings for their theater available on the tables or in the bar.

Positive word of mouth is the best advertising.

CHAPTER FIVE

PROMOTING YOUR RESTAURANT

Word of Mouth

Positive word of mouth is the best marketing and advertising there is, without question. But does it just come by accident or only from serving great food? Yes and no. Great word of mouth comes from guests having something great to talk about and sharing it effectively. Do you have a deliberate, creative and authentic plan in place to create great word of mouth? Guests don't talk about you unless they're thinking about you. You want them thinking about you in the right way, which means you have to educate your guests on why they come to you. To do this, you must create points of difference between you and your competitors. Then people can tell their friends about why they eat at your restaurant.

An effective word-of-mouth program has five main goals:

1. Inform and educate your patrons.
2. Make the guest a salesperson for your restaurant.
3. Give guests reasons to return.
4. Make your service unique and personal.
5. Distinguish your business from the competition.

- **Finally, always remember the winning formula:** Good Food + Extraordinary Service = Priceless Word-of-Mouth Marketing.

Getting To Know Your Guests - Market Yourself And Your Restaurant

In a business that lives and dies on personal connection, getting to know your guests is crucial. Go beyond the procedures of service; start thinking of your guests as individuals. There is a difference between serving 200 dinners and serving John and Betty Carson on their 30th wedding anniversary, or a doing fund-raiser for the Friends of the Community Theater. Numbers are important, but your relationship with your customers drives your business. The two easiest things to learn about your customers are also the most useful:

- **Who they are.** Do you have a system in place that teaches your new staff who these important folks are? You can train your servers to write the guest's name on the back of the check so they can refer to it throughout the meal. Alternatively, have your greeter put guests' names on their checks when they arrive. Continually remind waitstaff that they are serving people, not anonymous mouths. Using guests' names is another win-win proposition because the more you use their names, the easier they will be to remember and the easier it will be to treat them as individuals

- **What they like.** Now that you are talking to customers as individuals, the next step is to find out what they want as individuals. How? You must ask, but you also must remember, not only what you've been told, but also what you've observed. If you were allergic to a certain ingredient, wouldn't it be incredible if the next time you visited the restaurant, they offered to make you a dish that wasn't on the menu? If you loved the food but were seated too close to the air conditioner, wouldn't it be great if you were seated away from it next time?

Exceptional Service - One of Your Best Marketing Tools

What can ruin a fabulous meal for your guests and ensure that they won't be back? Bad service! The food industry suffers from a higher-than-average employee turnover rate. Keeping the quality of service exceptional is a difficult and constant task. Your restaurant is made up of two things in the eyes of your customers: the food and the staff. The quality of service your customers receive will determine their opinion of your restaurant. Here's how to impress your customers with your superlative service:

- **Develop guest service checklists.** In order to improve your service, you need to find out where you are weakest. A guest service checklist can help you make an accurate evaluation. Make a list of everything involved in a customer's experience, then have your staff members go through the checklist after working with a customer to see which areas they may need to improve upon next time.

- **Develop a strategic service mission.** A strategic service mission (SSM) is simply a guarantee you make to your customers about the quality or speed of your service. A good example is lunch in 30 minutes or less. Once you have an SSM, you can use it to generate publicity for your restaurant.

- **Maximize efficiency of scheduling.** Scheduling is one of the most difficult parts of your or your manager's job. Creating an efficient schedule involves knowing your employees. Use computer software to save you time and money such as Employee Schedule Partner at www.atlantic-pub.com.

- **Accept reservations.** Some restaurants have a strict first-come-first-served policy and refuse to accept reservations. If you don't want to fill up your dining area with reserved tables, consider setting aside a section on the busy evenings or at lunch times for individuals who want to call ahead. You may only want to take reservations for special occasions or from regular customers, but either way you should consider accepting at least some reservations.

- **Encourage call parties.** For those unfamiliar with the term, a "call party" is a guest who specifically requests a particular server for their dining experience. When a guest makes such a request, it obviously means that his or her last experience was something special. Encourage your servers to tell guests to ask for them by name during their next visit. You may even give servers business cards to distribute to customers.

Happy Hour

Happy Hour has been neglected by restaurants in recent years, but you can use that time for some prime marketing. Consider the following possibilities:

- Provide sample-size portions of entrées. For

example, instead of serving the traditional finger foods and appetizers, serve sample-size portions of your entrées. Once people taste how delicious your food is, they'll be more inclined to stick around for dinner or to come back for a meal in the near future.

- **Give away shelled shrimp.** Another way to inspire terrific word-of-mouth advertising is to give away something of a high-perceived value during Happy Hour. One example is shelled shrimp. Shelled shrimp is usually inexpensive and, because they are difficult to eat, patrons won't consume them in high numbers. But, it will give them something to talk about!

- **Provide light dinner.** Instead of offering Happy Hour drink specials, consider charging regular price but offering a light dinner buffet for free. Include finger foods and similar inexpensive items. This plan will appeal especially to busy singles who don't want to cook for themselves after a day at the office.

Lunch-Hour Opportunities

The key to maximizing lunchtime opportunities is to give your customers exactly what they want; quality fare served speedily and efficiently and at a reasonable price. Bear in mind the following factors when trying to please the lunch-hour crowd:

- **Offer time limits for lunch service.** Because most of your lunch crowd will be dealing with time constraints of 30 minutes to 1 hour, you should be especially time conscious. When Pizza Hut first starting catering to the lunch crowd with its

Personal Pan pizzas, it offered a 30-minute guarantee. The server even placed a timer on lunch patrons' tables. If it took longer, the food was free. You may want to consider implementing a similar lunchtime strategy. Just make sure that your staff is capable of meeting the deadline consistently or you'll lose a lot of money.

- Develop lunch specials. If you plan on doing business with companies in your area, you'll want to come up with some enticing lunch specials. Specials typically include smaller-sized versions of entrées and beverages. Imaginative sandwiches and salads are also very popular. You may also want to consider creating a frequent diner club (discussed in a later chapter) to increase lunch business.

- **Call businesses to announce lunch specials.** Encourage your servers to help market your lunch specials. Ask them to come in around 9:30 or 10 a.m. to start phoning surrounding businesses with your daily lunch specials. They can also ensure their own share of the success by asking these potential customers to request him or her by name when they come in for lunch. Also, make sure they pitch any guarantees you have about service, such as lunch in 30 minutes or it's free.

- **Visit local businesses with samples.** If you want to bring in a sizable lunch crowd, this is a great idea. Go around to nearby businesses (you may want to call ahead first) and pass out samples to everyone you encounter. Invite them to pay you a visit, pass out brochures, give directions and tell them about the specials. You will have a captive audience as long as your samples last. You will see some of them for lunch.

- **Implement a lunchtime delivery program.** Many people may love to come to your restaurant for lunch, but they may simply not have the time. Consider implementing a lunchtime delivery program to surrounding employers. You may want to create a limited menu of easily transportable food and then fax, mail or drop off copies to all of the locations you plan to service. You may also want to call a few offices and let them know you are making deliveries. Definitely set a minimum order, perhaps at least three items and guarantee delivery by the time their lunch break starts. Your Web site could be set up to take orders as well. In each lunch you deliver, include information on your Happy Hour or dinner specials, maybe even a coupon.

- **Discontinue lunch service on weekends.** The idea of your lunch specials is to motivate area workers to visit your restaurant regularly. During the weekend that is no longer an issue. By continuing to have lunch specials on Saturdays and Sundays, you only lose profits.

Special Occasions

Special occasions provide a major opportunity to promote your restaurant. Here are some ideas to help you make the most of the occasion:

- **Keep a "house" Polaroid camera.** When people come for a special event, they don't always remember to bring their own camera. Have a staff member with a Polaroid camera walk around to take a picture of the fun. Use a Polaroid or digital camera because the pictures will be developed instantly. Make sure to take an extra picture to post on your special-event wall and Web site.

- **Send personal notes to large parties.** When your restaurant hosts large parties (more than 10 people), make sure to send the hostess or person who made the arrangements a handwritten note thanking them for their business and making sure that everything went smoothly. You may want to include a small survey and even a thank-you voucher for their next visit, or a photo of the event in a small paper frame with your restaurant and date on the side.

- **Offer private dining rooms.** Many people want to have a special night out, but they don't relish the idea of being surrounded by noisy people having their own good time. This is especially true for anniversaries, marriage proposals and Valentine's Day dinners. Set aside an area for private dining. You should make it a reservation-only section, however, so when it is not reserved you can open it up to the regular crowd.

- **Start a birthday club.** Birthday clubs don't have to be just for children. When a guest joins, be sure to send them a personalized birthday card in time for their special day along with a voucher for a free dessert, drink or meal (your choice). Also, make sure to add them to your regular mailing list.

- **Use a scrolling board to announce special occasions.** Place your scrolling board where guests can see it, then use it to wish greetings to birthday guests or other diners celebrating each evening. Remember, a celebration doesn't have to be a traditional event; it can be a job promotion, a new baby, good grades, etc.

- **Offer special-event reminder service.** This service is great especially for people too busy to remember birthdays and anniversaries. To join, the regular guest completes a form including important events they are afraid of missing. Then, about a week before that date, send out a reminder and a discount coupon so they can take that special someone to dinner at your establishment. You can even go a step further and send cards to the birthday boy or girl yourself along with a coupon for something free with a note saying "A gift from (Your Restaurant's Name) and (Guest's Name) for your (special event)." You can also automate this process by using e-mail and a database program.

- **Make a limo available.** For special occasions, such as birthdays, anniversaries, marriage proposals and prom dates, limo service may be the perfect addition to a wonderful evening. You may want to form an arrangement with a limo service in your area. Guests will need to schedule the evening in advance. You may want to add a fee for the limo service to the cost of the bill. Make sure to publicize this service. Another option would be horse-drawn carriage rides.

- **Make souvenirs available.** People love to have something by which to remember their special occasion. Consider including souvenirs with their meal or making them available for purchase. The souvenir should have some connection to your restaurant so they'll remember their experience every time they see it. Visit sites such as www.myron.com, www.ahrpromotions.com and www.tagdesigns.com to get an idea of what is available.

Promotions, Promotions, Promotions

One of the easiest ways to increase your customer base is by luring diners in with contests, discounts and good publicity. Chances are you'll only get one shot to make the right impression, so the long-lasting impact of these promotions depends on what happens in your restaurant once they get inside. Consider the following possibilities:

- **Nightly free-meal drawing.** A great way to fill up your restaurant on a Monday or Tuesday night is with a free-meal drawing. The key, however, is not to advertise the contest. Let customers' word-of-mouth marketing spread the word for you. At a certain time on each of those nights (the time should be undisclosed and should change every week) randomly select a table or even a seat. The winner receives their meal that evening for free.

- **Give away a private dinner**. If you're looking for a fabulous prize for your next contest, consider giving away a private dinner. The dinner can be for as many people as you care to make it (anywhere from two to eight) and should include an appetizer, entrées, dessert and tea or coffee. You will want to specify that alcoholic beverages are not included. You may also want to consider having customers use their receipts as entry forms so you can make sure that your regular clients have the advantage.

- **Regular business-card drawing.** This contest is a great way to build up your mailing list and to boost your lunch crowd. You can either have a container at the front of your restaurant or you could have a server go around the dining area informing patrons of the contest and asking them to drop in their business cards. Then, every week or every month, select a card to receive a free lunch. Another possible prize is a free lunch for the cardholder and up to five of his or her co-workers. From these cards, you can find out information about your individual customers, but you'll also be able to identify how far your lunch crowd is traveling to get to you so you can adjust your promotions accordingly.

- **Day-with-the-chef contest.** Most diners never get an opportunity to meet the chefs at their favorite restaurants, let alone see how they create all of those fabulous meals. You might want to consider centering a contest around him or her. The winner could spend the day assisting the chef, then be rewarded with a specialized dish just for them that they've helped to cook. You may want to organize this contest on special occasions, perhaps to celebrate your chef's anniversary with your restaurant.

- **Hold an adult "Easter egg hunt."** Easter egg hunts aren't just for children. People love the suspense of searching for a prize. The fun is the anticipation. Have the server bring out the plastic egg with the chook. Place a variety of prizes including dollar bills, coupons, free meals or lottery tickets. Your customers will love the possibility of winning something and will come back again for another chance.

- **Hold a customer-idea contest.** You want to do something different at your restaurant; change the decor, add a new menu item, make a brand new drink, but you don't have any ideas. Hold a customer-idea contest. Ask your guests to submit their ideas into a fishbowl (or suggestion box), along with their names, addresses and phone numbers (use this info for your mailing list). Then, if you choose to implement any of the ideas – and you should try to use at least one or two – you can reward the customer who made the suggestion with a free meal or some other prize. You will also want to publicize that the idea came from a customer; it will give you good press and loyal customers.

- **Send non-winners a prize for entering.** Obviously, with any contest, some individuals will be winners and most won't, right? Not necessarily. Even those who don't win the main prizes should still receive some sort of gift to thank them for entering and to encourage them to enter next time. Consider sending a personalized letter to each non-winner along with a voucher for a free dessert or appetizer that they can redeem on their next visit.

- **Hold children's contests.** Include children by having special contests just for them. You can use coloring contests, guessing contests (e.g., how many jelly beans are in the jar), trivia games or raffles. However, children won't recognize the value of a free meal, so you'll need to create prizes that they'll want to win: toys, gift certificates, movie coupons, amusement park tickets, video tapes, etc.

Create a Fun "Event"

There's nothing like a fun event for drumming up interest. It provides a great way of advertising your restaurant at minimal costs. Here are some ideas:

- **Bring in a variety of entertainment.** Give your customers a reason not to go anywhere else. Bring in karaoke music, comedians, local bands, poetry readings or piano players. The only limits are space, availability and your imagination. Make sure to promote the entertainment for at least two weeks in advance to give customers a chance to work you into their plans. The easiest way to get hold of some form of entertainment is to place ads in the newspaper or place flyers around college campuses, bookstores, music shops, etc. As for karaoke systems, you may be able to find them locally at music stores or you could shop online at a site such as www.acekaraoke.com that has both home and professional systems for sale.

- **Start a food festival.** A restaurant is all about the food, right? So why not celebrate it? Pick a particular ingredient and make as many creative dishes with it as possible. You can choose something simple like potatoes or something more exotic, such as oysters. Then, make sure to include all those dishes on a special Food Festival menu for a week or a month. Make sure to keep serving your old favorites as well, but hype up the new dishes. At the end of the festival, you can have customers vote on one of the dishes to be added to the regular menu.

- **Celebrate your restaurant's anniversary.** While most people celebrate their anniversary by being guests of honor at a party and by receiving gifts, when your establishment's anniversary rolls around, you need to make sure that you make it a party for your customers. After all, they're the ones who got you this far. Offer specials, such as discounted appetizers or free desserts, or create new menu items. Hold contests. Bring in entertainment. Give out balloons, party favors, etc. The idea is to make your restaurant fun and to thank your customers for their patronage.

- **Create a "wooden nickel war" with your competition.** You will need to work with your competition on this one. People get excited by competition; use that excitement to your advantage. The wooden nickel (actually it can be coupons, cards or any small item) entitles the bearer to a free drink from the bar. What you need to do with these wooden nickels is to go into your competitor's restaurant and pass them out to the guests. Your competitor then retaliates. If you conduct these games on busy nights, you're sure to have the whole city talking about your antics, which will arouse curiosity and boost business for both you and your competition.

- **Hold a spontaneous competition.** If you have a couple of really outgoing servers or staff members, this idea works great and creates a real feeling of spontaneity in your restaurant. The idea is that your two staff members challenge each other right there in your dining area. What they challenge each other to is up to you. You may have servers race across the dining room with an egg on a spoon or a tray of plastic wine glasses filled with confetti. Let the guests decide the winner.

- **Hold appreciation nights for community members**. Most communities are full of people who make valuable contributions but often go unappreciated, such as teachers, fire fighters, police officers, secretaries, etc. Consider rectifying that by holding a special recognition night for them. You can offer them a free dinner (they'll bring guests who will buy their own food and drinks) and provide them with some small token of appreciation. Not only will you receive media attention for the event, but those whom you honor will reward you with their loyal patronage as well.

- **Hold invite-only taste testing.** Once you have a mailing list of your loyal customers, you may want to consider holding invite-only events, such as a taste-testing party. Invite customers to attend the event by sending out invitations with RSVP. You supply the food samples, tea, coffee and water, but have a bartender available to fill their drink orders. Ask them for their opinions and then select the items that receive the best responses. On your menu, you may even want to mention that the new items were selected by a panel of loyal customers.

- **Hold a global food festival.** A global food festival is where you pick a particular culture's recipes. Mexican, Italian, French and Chinese foods all work well, but you may want to be a little more adventurous. What about Japanese cuisine or dishes from Eastern Europe? As an alternative, you could also offer food from a variety of cultures on a buffet so that customers get an opportunity to taste an assortment of dishes they may never have tried.

- **Put the competition to the test**. Another fun idea is to hold a cook-off with some of your competing restaurants. Offer to hold the event at your establishment (so you get the home-court advantage) and let the customers decide. You can either charge a simple admission to cover your expenses or you can charge for beverages, either way you'll make a profit. Another option is to hold the competition at local gatherings, such as fairs, sporting events, car shows, etc. While beating the competition would be a great way to end the event, your primary objective is just to give customers an experience they'll remember and to make sure they have an opportunity to taste your delicious food and walk away with your promotional material.

- **Special event.** Pick a special occasion for your restaurant: St. Patrick's Day, Super Bowl Sunday, your restaurant's anniversary, etc. For about one to two months prior to that big day, run a promotion: every time a guest comes in and spends $10/$20/$30 dollars (you pick the amount), reward him or her with $1 in special-event dollars. Then, on the day of this big event, these guests can bring in the dollars they've accumulated and use them towards their purchase. It's a good way to bring guests back frequently during that period and to ensure a full house for the big event. Community events typically get a lot of press. If you can become a part of those events, you will benefit from that publicity. You could be a sponsor or an announcer. You could provide food and refreshments or help with the fundraising. You could simply help by promoting the event in your establishment. No matter how you participate, the people in the community, those same people who are your customers, will think of you as a valuable member of the town and will show their appreciation by frequenting your restaurant. Here are some more suggestions for involving your restaurant with the local community:

- **Make friends with local radio stations.** Buy a whole advertising package with a live remote broadcast. Most stations have mobile units that visit clubs, concerts and restaurants and host their broadcasts. You may also want to provide prizes for station contests and giveaways as well.

- **Offer to help three people who need your services.** Nothing attracts positive media attention like helping those who are less fortunate, especially around the holidays. Find three people or three families who cannot afford to dine at your restaurant, or any restaurant for that matter, and provide them with a wonderful meal free of charge. Imagine how it will look the next morning when a story on your good deed is featured in the local newspaper.

- **Enter contests.** What is one of the best reasons to create a press release? Because you've just won a contest! But how are you going to win those contests? First, you need to enter every contest you can find. You'll find these contests in publications dedicated to the restaurant and food industry. Even if you don't win in a national competition, simply entering or finishing with an honorable mention is worthy of a release. If you're located in a small- to medium-size town, you can invite the media to see or taste your entry before you submit it, which will provide additional coverage.

- **Donate your product.** In schools, businesses and throughout the community, there are opportunities for you to donate your product. You may include coupons in a discount book for students to sell, give rewards that businesses can give to employees or offer prizes for contests held by local organizations. Donating your product has a twofold benefit: You receive a great deal of positive publicity and those who receive your donated product will come in and spend money as will their guests. Plus, all of your donations are tax deductible.

- **Hold a canned food drive.** Many restaurants have not only achieved great press by holding an event such as this, but they have also seen a dramatic increase in business. Simply reward guests who bring in a canned food item. You may give them a free item or a discount or enter them into a special drawing. After your event is a success, make sure to credit the success solely to your customers who came out and supported it. If they feel good about what they did, they'll feel good about eating at your establishment as well. Get pictures and use in your newsletter and on your Web site.

CHAPTER SIX

MARKETING YOUR RESTAURANT TO KIDS, PARENTS & FAMILIES

Kid-Friendly Ideas

Until recently, the only restaurants that were primarily concerned with pleasing kids were fast food chains and that was limited to including a small toy with the purchase of a hamburger.

Now, a dining experience at the Outback, Chili's or Olive Garden are weekly family events, and in many cases, the children have at least an equal say in choosing where those families spend their food dollars. If you don't create an amazing experience for the twelve-and-under crowd, you won't get their vote. How do you make sure the kids are campaigning for you? Here are a few suggestions:

- **Always have a kids' menu.** There was a time when children seldom saw the inside of a nice restaurant. Not anymore. Parents today are taking their children along, which makes a children's menu essential. Without one, parents will feel pressured to pay full price for a meal their children may not like and will definitely not finish. They will be unlikely to return. Keep in mind that children have a lot to do with family dining decisions, so meeting their needs is just as important as satisfying their parents'.

- **Use small versions of adult entrées for children.** What to put on those children's menus may seem like a tough question. Most places go for the usual hamburgers, grilled cheese, hot dogs and macaroni and cheese. But think of it this way: those children will grow up one day and become adult diners who no longer order from the under-12 menu. Wouldn't it be great if you could convince those young diners now that they loved your steak or your fettuccine Alfredo? In addition to one or two traditional offerings, consider filling out your children's menu with smaller versions of adult favorites: steaks, pasta and fajitas. You will win a lifetime patron.

- **No charge for kids' meals.** One of the easiest ways to win over families is by offering free kids' meals with the purchase of an adult entrée. What better way to say your establishment embraces family business? Parents will love it and if you can also convince the children, you'll be on the tips of their tongues when it comes time to pick a restaurant.

- **Use their names.** Adult customers enjoy personal recognition, so why wouldn't their children? Servers should make a point of asking for their names early on and using it as often as possible. In fact, you could also have name tag stickers that the greeter could give them when they are seated. Children will feel special and important because of the extra attention.

- **Ask them what they want.** Many servers just automatically ask parents to order for their children, but older kids will feel slighted by being overlooked. The server should ask the child for his or her order, then glance at the parents to get their approval. In most situations, the parents and the child have consulted about their order already. When it comes to desserts, however, do not address the child until the parents express an interest in ordering one. Otherwise, you could inadvertently create a problem for the parents which they won't appreciate.

- **Give them small gifts.** Children love presents, even small ones. Crayons are a popular favorite, so are stickers. You can find a variety of toys and place them in a bucket or box, then let each child select one at the end of his or her meal. Make sure that the toys are age appropriate; you don't want to give anything that is a potential choking hazard. Also avoid candy, since many children are not allowed to have it. Party stores, teacher resource shops, even toy stores in your area will have a plethora of small, inexpensive items you can buy in bulk.

- **Use small flatware.** Young kids will feel special having their own fork to eat with and it will be a lot easier for them.

- **Give free balloons.** As little ones exit the restaurant, you can hand them a balloon with your restaurant's name and logo on it. They'll have something to remember the experience by and you'll get some free advertising as well. Sites such as www.tagdesigns.com or www.arhpromotions.com make it easy and inexpensive for you to order in bulk.

- **Make a survey just for them**. One of your chief goals is to evaluate how satisfied your customers are with your food and service, so why not design a survey for the kids as well? They'll love the opportunity to give their feedback, plus you'll be surprised at the quality of the ideas and suggestions they'll provide.

- **Photo opportunities.** Most children love getting their picture taken almost as much as they love eating candy. Provide lots of photo opportunities. For holidays, have the Easter Bunny and Santa Claus around for pictures. During the spring and summer, consider bringing a pony or other small animal to your parking lot for snapshots with guests' children. Consider posting some of the pictures up in the restaurant and your Web site so children will want to come back and see their pictures again, as will the parents. Don't have a Web site? Get one today!

- **Create family packs.** Family packs are another way of welcoming family business. Many fast food restaurants already use it. For example, Kentucky Fried Chicken offers 10 pieces of chicken with all the sides and the biscuits for one low price. The idea is to provide enough food for a family at one price. Homestyle cooking establishments do this as well by offering one meat, vegetables and rolls all for one price. You could create a similar deal in almost any other restaurant as well; an appetizer, two adult entrées, two children's meals and two desserts for one price.

- **Provide wet towelettes.** Maybe the children won't appreciate this as much as the parents, but they'll prefer it to being sticky and messy until they get home.

- **Host family nights.** A family night is a great idea for a slow Monday or Tuesday. You may want to include discounts on kids' meals and have entertainment, such as family movies, musicians and magicians. The idea is to give families a good reason to dine out on an unusual night.

A Space of Their Own

Develop a separate children's dining/play area. Even though parents bring their children along to dinner, it doesn't mean they wouldn't appreciate a little break. You could section off part of your dining area just for kids. Give them their own servers and special decor. You could also put games, toys and books in the area to keep them busy while they wait for their food. Make sure you have good supervision for the area. If parents know their children are in good hands, they can relax, stay longer, order another glass of wine or a dessert and have a great evening. Also consider the following possibilities:

- **Create game rooms with tokens.** Typically, children finish eating before their parents. To keep little ones occupied while their parents finish their meals, you can create a game room. The room can include video games or games of skill (speedball, basketball, etc.) that will appeal to children. You can have the games take tokens instead of quarters and include several tokens with the child's meal. Extra tokens can be purchased from the server and simply added onto the total bill. As an extra bonus, you can give away prizes as well. You can find new or reconditioned stand-up arcade games, novelty games, skeet ball, air hockey tables and more online at sites such as www.skeeball.com and www.arcadegames.com.

- **Hire a "kid wrangler."** Essentially, a kid wrangler is someone you have on staff to keep the kids entertained. They may dress up like a clown or take kids on tours of the kitchen. They could perform magic tricks or juggle. The ideas are practically endless. Your kid wrangler does not have to be available every day, but you may want to have them available on weekend afternoons and on family nights. In fact, your kid wrangler could pull double duty as a greeter. A good way to find a qualified kid wrangler is to contact local colleges in your area that teach early education courses.

- **Create a children's mascot.** Promote your kid-friendly "space" by developing a children's mascot that fits in with the theme of your restaurant. For example, if you specialize in fish, you may want to have a dolphin or a pirate as a mascot.

- **Add a fish tank.** Have you ever watched the face of a child staring into a fish tank? Most can't take their eyes off the bright colors and the unusual fish. You may want to add one in the kids' "dining room." While the family waits for their meals, a server or greeter can take the children to view the fish tank so they won't become bored and disruptive.

- **Hold coloring contests in the kids' space.** Children love coloring contests! You can hold this regularly, perhaps even monthly. As prizes, you can give gift certificates to your restaurant or coupons for free meals or desserts. Not only will you be making the kids happy, you'll be giving them a reason to come back.

Using the School

Involving your local school is great fun. It is also an excellent way to market your restaurant in the community. Here are some ideas that will appeal to teachers, pupils and parents:

- **Consider going to local schools and having a cooking show.** You can bring your top cook and demonstrate to students how your restaurant makes its gooey desserts and scrumptious appetizers. Bring some of the kids on stage to participate. Afterward, distribute a sheet of kid-friendly recipes and a coupon for a free kids' meal at your restaurant.

- **Sponsor school activities.** Most local schools have sports teams, academic programs and other extracurricular activities that need volunteers and sponsors. By pitching in at a school in the vicinity of your restaurant, you are showing that you are a caring member of the community and you are getting your name out to hundreds of potentially hungry parents and teachers.

- **Reward good grades.** Students who get good grades on their progress reports are always looking for a way to celebrate, so offer them a little extrinsic motivation. Offer free desserts or free kids' meals for a job well done. Make sure to promote your offer by contacting the local schools or by distributing certificates to teachers.

- **Participate in coupon fund-raisers.** Many schools sell coupon books to raise money for activities, supplies or new equipment. Volunteer to participate in as many of these as possible. Not only will your participation be a great source of advertising, the parents will come to your restaurant to redeem their coupons.

- **Share profits.** Another popular fund-raiser for schools in recent years is to partner with a nearby retail store or restaurant. The students are given slips to distribute to family members, parents' co-workers and neighbors. Then, on a given day (usually a weekday), for every person who brings in their slip and purchases dinner, a certain percentage (10-20 percent) of their purchase will go back to the school. It's a great way to boost business on a slow night while giving back to the community.

- **Consider a school lunch program.** While not every school district allows private providers to participate in the lunch programs, you may at least be able to add some of your products or bid on performing the entire function. Contact your local school district food service director to inquire about the possibilities.

CHAPTER SEVEN

EXTERNAL MARKETING

Your Restaurant is Different - Get the Message Across!

Having a great idea in place, such as the many listed in this manual, isn't enough! You've got to inform your customers about it and give them the words they can then pass on. How do you get this information across? Here's the secret:

- **Arm your staff with words they can comfortably work into a conversation.** Do you offer a full menu until midnight? When guests call and ask how late you're open, say, "Dave's Cafe serves a full menu until midnight. We're the only place in town that does." If a guest comes in at 11:00 p.m. wondering if you're still open, say, "Not only are we open, we serve a full menu until closing at midnight." Over time your customers will be saying "Dave's serves a full menu until midnight. Let's go there."

- **If you give your customers a great experience and the words to describe it, they'll talk about it to their friends.** A customer telling his friends he had a great time is great. A customer telling his friends he had the best salad ever because you have an organic garden in the back and the lettuce was picked 5 minutes before his salad was prepared is worth its weight in gold. Details differentiate your product and make yours the place to go for something extraordinary.

Most of this manual is dedicated to internal marketing, which are the efforts you make within your business in order to spread the word, such as updating your menu or sponsoring a contest. These are probably not the type of changes you think of when you hear the term "marketing," but in reality it's about 75 percent of the marketing in which you'll engage. The remaining 25 percent is external marketing, such as advertisements, press releases, etc. Grasp the basics about advertising; your restaurant will not survive without them:

- **Follow the KISS principle.** KISS is an acronym meaning "Keep It Simple, Stupid." In a nutshell, this should be the guiding idea behind all of your advertising. Your message must be easy to understand for the average customer. It should also be brief. No one is going to read two pages of text just to learn that you have a great seafood buffet.

- **Advertise all the time.** Even if business is steady and you're happy with your current profit share, never let up on advertising. Many businesses make the mistake of stopping their advertising when business is good. But bear in mind that today's ad is really generating business for the next six months! How do you know that business will be this good in six months? Keeping yourself in the minds of potential customers will help you maintain your momentum, which is ultimately what you want for long-term success.

- **Choose an appropriate medium.** When you decide to advertise, the first decision you need to make is about the medium you will use. This decision is influenced by two factors: budget and audience. Television commercials are more expensive than radio spots; newspaper ads are cheaper than billboards, so you pick the medium(s) that you can afford. Newspaper ads work well for older audiences. Billboards may be great to attract tourists. Television commercials will usually be perfect for family business. Make a list of the clientele you want to attract with the ad and decide how much you can budget, narrow down your options and start getting pricing. Never enter any long-term ad agreements until you've tested them. You don't want to be stuck with a billboard that doesn't bring you business for a year.

- **Write a creative brief.** Before you decide on an advertising campaign, you need to produce a creative brief. This short document just outlines some of the important information you'll need as you design and implement an effective ad strategy. The brief needs to include your target audience, your evaluation method and your budget constraints as well as an examination of what your customers already know about you, what you want them to get from the ad and what you intend to accomplish.

- **Remember the three-mile rule.** When you are planning advertising of any kind, remember this general rule: your customers will come to you from within a three-mile radius. Setting up a billboard ten miles away won't be an effective use of your ad dollars. Instead, take out a map of your town and determine your circle of influence. All of your sales, advertising and PR efforts should be focused within that area.

- **Remember the noon-until-5 rule.** Similar to the rule above, this one focuses just on the customers you're going to deal with around lunch time and in the early afternoon. These customers, generally, will travel no more than 5 minutes to get to your restaurant. Before you start sending out flyers about lunch specials or faxing reservations for Happy Hour, make sure all of your potential customers are within a 5-minute drive of your location. Otherwise, you may want to save your stamp.

- **Use effective images.** Most of your ads will include some sort of image. The image you choose has a great deal of impact on whether or not that particular ad succeeds or fails. Most advertising experts agree that there are 11 types of images that work best. However, not all of these work well with restaurants. You might want to consider using pictures of your food, satisfied customers, before/after photos (bored family dining at home/laughing family at your restaurant) and product comparisons.

- **Develop a logo.** Logos are a great way to give your restaurant a little personality. They don't have to be fancy, but they do need to be eye-catching and something you can use consistently on your menus, in your decor, on your sales materials, on your business cards, etc. One way to get your logo done inexpensively is to work with local artists. You may want to approach one about doing your logo in exchange for displaying their work in your restaurant. Graphic design students may also offer you a reduced rate and good-quality work so that they'll have something for their professional portfolio. One great freelance graphic artist we highly recommend is Megadesign, www.mega-designs.com, e-mail: megadesn@mhtc.net.

- **Develop a catchy tag line.** No logo is complete without a great tag line. Remember Wendy's slogan in the 1980s, "Where's the Beef?" Even today, people remember that line and associate it with their restaurant. Your tag line may not be able to produce that level of response, but if it's memorable, your establishment will be too. For example, "The Place Where Friends Meet" or "Wings Are Us."

- **Demand advertising accountability.** With any advertising you do, you need to expect results. You are spending your valuable dollars to boost your business, so you need to know if it's doing the job. Don't just assume that an influx of customers means they've seen your ad and loved it. Ask customers how they heard of you. Find out if they've seen your ads and what they think of them. Actively pursue their feedback. If you discover that your current ad isn't working, abandon it and try something else. Once you find something that does work, stick with it for awhile. When business starts to reach equilibrium, start all over again.

Advertising Specifics

The following ideas will help you make the most of those valuable, external marketing dollars:

- **List your business in phone directories.** When people are looking for a restaurant, the phone book may not be the first place they look for ideas. But if they're new in town, visiting or looking for something a little different, chances are they'll browse through the Yellow Pages. If you're not there, they won't know you exist. Also, make sure to list yourself in the White Pages.

- **Leave brochures for tourists.** How many times have you been on vacation looking for a great place to get a bite to eat but found nothing but fast food chains along the way? Wouldn't it have been nice if you could have stopped at a gas station and found some brochures for local restaurants along with those for the zoo, museums and amusement parks in the surrounding area? A brochure with pictures and text can be produced inexpensively on most desktop computers using only the software that comes packaged with it and a scanner or digital camera (for the pictures). However, if you can afford it, by all means have one professionally done. Leave them at gas stations, doctors' offices, the post office or DMV (any place where people have to wait in boredom). Make sure to include detailed directions, hours of operation and your phone number in the brochure to make it easy for customers to find you.

- **Include hours of operation.** As mentioned above, you should always include your hours of operation. Not just on brochures, however, but on any type of advertising or sales material you create. Many restaurants don't serve breakfast, others don't open until early evening, while a few stay open very late. If you don't advertise your hours, people will have to guess. If they want something to eat at midnight, they'll just assume you're not open for business and instead will go somewhere they know stays open late.

- **Place an ad on a billboard.** A billboard can be very effective for advertising your food, especially if you place it rather close to your restaurant. Seeing a platter of fresh chicken or a juicy steak in full color hovering above the road is enough to make some drivers and passengers suddenly realize they're starving. If the billboard is close enough, you can even include directions, such as "turn right at the next light" so your potential clients won't have to look too hard to find you. However, they are typically pricey and long-term, so consider them only if they fit into your budget and you're positive your ad will work.

- **List your company in business directories.** While diners may not be browsing business directories to find a place for lunch, business professionals will be scanning them for places to hold meetings or to visit while in town for work. Also, your listing may cause you to be approached about forming strategic alliances or cross-promotional events.

- **Leave materials with visitors' bureaus.** When visitors come to your city, there's a good chance they've already contacted your visitors' bureau or will pay them a visit. Your materials can be displayed along with other tourist attractions, so as they browse for a brochure on the local zoo, they'll also come across you; a nice alternative to all of the fast food chains along the road or airline food.

- **Use flyers.** Flyers are cheap to produce and easy to distribute. All you need is a pack of brightly colored paper and a computer. Use them to announce entertainment, specials, new products, events, etc. Make the print large and easy to read, then print off plenty. You can pass them out at your restaurant, hand them out at public places, even pin them to light poles. Just remember to distribute them within your three-mile circle of influence.

- **Place ads in malls, bathrooms and near ATMs.** One of the latest trends is to place ads in unusual places, such as in bathrooms. The idea is perfect. Imagine being in the bathroom of your local movie theater after the film is finished, you look up at the back of the door and see several ads. Obviously, you're a captive audience so you read the ads. The ads also work well outside of the bathroom stalls where people often have to wait in a line with nothing to occupy them but the wallpaper. If your ad is that wallpaper, then they're looking at you.

- **Use vanity plates.** Make your car a tax write-off by using vanity plates to advertise your restaurant. Obviously, this won't work with all restaurant names, but if you're creative, you can make it work. If you don't want to use the name, consider using your chief product or simply saying "Chef." The idea is to attract attention to yourself, then when someone asks you about the plate, you give them the spiel about your restaurant, whip out a business card listing your restaurant's address and tell them to drop by soon for a great meal. Works great!

- **Test ads.** This is so important, especially to small businesses. Obviously, your advertising budget is limited. If you design an ad and start a campaign around that ad, then find out that it doesn't work, you've lost a lot of valuable money. You can minimize that loss by testing all of your ads beforehand. Put together a test group of employees and customers and let them evaluate the ad or send out a small sampling to a select area. Then monitor the response rate. If the results are positive, implement the campaign. If not, go back to the drawing board.

- **Develop a strategic alliance.** Let's say a man buys his girlfriend an engagement ring. What's the next step? Usually he takes her out to dinner, right? What about a couple staying at a hotel on vacation? Aren't they likely to go out to dinner at least once? These are just two possibilities for a strategic alliance. Essentially, you contact the jewelers, hotels, theaters, etc., in your area and interest them in promoting your restaurant. They might give every ring buyer a certificate for a free bottle of champagne or a free entrée, for example. In exchange, you promote them. Perhaps you allow them to sponsor (in name only) an event at your restaurant or you provide discounts for their services to your patrons. A good example was a locally owned fast food restaurant that gave free movie tickets to any customer who spent more than $20. What most customers didn't know was that the same person owned both the restaurant and the theater. Pretty clever!

- **Advertise in school/college newspapers.** Local newspapers aren't the only periodicals accepting ads these days. Many high school and college newspapers also use them. Generally, you can get better prices for ads in these papers, but the drawback (or plus, depending on your target audience) is that readership is fairly limited to young people. Both groups have relatively large disposable incomes and neither has the time (and in some cases, the desire) to spend hours slaving in the kitchen. Try it out for a month or so and track the success. You may be surprised.

- **Advertise on movie theater slides.** One of the latest advertisement gimmicks is showing at your local multiplex. Before the movie, even before the previews, guests are being bombarded with advertisements on the big screen. Many of the ads come from large companies, such as Pepsi, but most theaters also show ads for local companies. Contact the management of cinemas in your area (the ones closest to your restaurant are preferable) to find out pricing, which varies, and other requirements.

- **Get testimonials from local celebrities.** People don't always trust their own judgment, which is why they are always interested in what others have to say about stores, movies, music and food. The more they trust the person, the more likely they are to listen. Get some endorsements from local celebrities: favorite teachers, the mayor, media personalities, local reporters, etc. Invite them to your restaurant for a fabulous dinner and then get their comments. Make sure, however, you have their permission in writing before you use their feedback in any type of promotion.

- **Use paycheck stuffers.** Most individuals are more receptive to advertising when they are in a positive, upbeat mood. Why not advertise at a time that makes almost everyone happier than usual – pay day? Place a coupon or discount offer in the paychecks of local businesses. Contact the human resources department of the companies. You may want to focus on one company per week so you can see which ones deliver the best results. If the HR people seem reluctant, pay them a visit with samples or send them a gift basket.

- **Advertise on mobile transportation.** Ads are everywhere today! Busses, taxis, subways – all types of mobile transportation seem to be sporting one or two. Don't miss out on the opportunity. Prices vary depending on the size of the ad, type of transportation, etc., so you'll need to call around in your area for estimates before making a decision. If you do choose to advertise in this medium, make sure to include a full-color picture of the best-looking food your restaurant offers.

Technology

The most recent external market development has been the rise of the World Wide Web and the Web site. Here are some ideas for making the most of the Internet and technology communications to advertise your restaurant.

- **Create a Web site.** Since your primary goal won't be to conduct business over the Internet, your site won't need to be fancy or complicated. Your site will need to provide the restaurant's background, photos of your food, directions and contact information, plus details about upcoming events, etc. Press releases and newsletters are nice additions as well. You may consider adding a shopping section where you can sell products with your logo or packaged versions of your most popular entrées. For a great Web design firm that specializes in restaurants, contact Gizmo Graphics at www.gizwebs.com.

- **Submit your Web site to search engines.** Once you have that Web site, you will need to submit it to search engines. You've put effort into it and possibly money, so you want people to see it. Some

Web design companies will handle the submission process for you. If you have to do it yourself, simply go to the search engine sites (Yahoo.com, MSN.com, Google.com, etc.) and look near the bottom of the page for a link to their Web site-submission section. Carefully read the requirements before completing the forms. Your site won't instantly appear in the engine results; it usually takes anywhere from a few days to several months.

- **Build an e-mail database.** Once you have a Web site, you can use it to collect e-mail addresses from individuals who visit your site. You can also gather e-mail addresses from your regular customers as well by requesting them on contest entries and customer surveys or by gathering them from business cards. With these addresses, create a database and a mailing list. You can use e-mail to send out a four-color newsletter about your customers, employees, contests, promotions or specials. You will be saving a great deal in postage and time and it is instant.

- **Publish articles online.** One way to use the Internet to get a little publicity is to write an article and have it published online. Many sites have newsletters or e-zines (electronic magazines) that use articles. Some sites use them as content as well. You may want to search for restaurant-related sites, find out which accept articles, print their guidelines (usually posted on the site or available by mail), then write your article. If published, make sure to include a resource box listing your name and information about your restaurant. You may even want to write a press release announcing the publication to your local media. For information about food e-zines, see www.ezine-dir.com/Food.

- **Provide pre-recorded entertainment for customers on hold.** When customers call, it is inevitable that they will have to be put on hold at some point. People hate being put on hold as much as, if not more than, they hate standing in long lines, so make the time enjoyable. Instead of the normal "elevator music" that most companies play, pre-record a clever ad, a series of jokes or detailed descriptions of your food for callers to listen to until your staff can get back to them.

- **Have closed competitors' calls forwarded to you.** The cafe down the street went out of business. What are you going to do? Well, you might want to contact the phone company and request that the calls to their number be forwarded to you, or pick up their number. When potential customers dial up the now-defunct restaurant, they'll instead get you who will give them the unfortunate news and invite them to try your place instead.

- **Convert menu into a pdf for Web site.** Here's another idea for your Web site: you can convert your existing menu into a pdf document (requires Adobe Acrobat) which you can place on the site. Then visitors can view and even download your entire menu online. The advantage of the pdf format is that it provides security options that can prevent cut-and-paste plagiarism, plus it preserves the professional, crisp look of the menu.

- **Fax specials to nearby businesses.** While once only used by larger businesses, fax machines have become so affordable that even consumers have them. Call local businesses (in your 5-minute area) and ask if they would like you to fax them a copy of your daily lunch specials. It's an easy way to get the word out to the lunch crowd. But get their permission first. Should your fax list get big enough, you can fax directly from your computer using fax transmission software or a service bureau that will take your art file and database and send the fax out for you. There are also services that will take your incoming faxes and convert them into e-mails for you to receive. The advantage is you can do this without tying up your fax line. You could receive 20 lunch orders by e-mail all at the same time. The customer will never get a busy signal.

- **Fax abbreviated menus and order forms.** Another way to use that fax machine is to send abbreviated menus (one to two pages, brief descriptions, no pictures) along with an order form. The business can write down everyone's order and fax it back to you. Then, you can either deliver the orders to their business or have them ready when they arrive hungry for lunch. Either way, you'll be making it easier for them to decide where to spend that valuable hour. Again, get their permission first.

Sales Materials

The following guidelines for creating winning sales copy could make all the difference between the success and failure of your marketing strategy:

- **Use the nine components of effective copy.** If you're writing your own sales copy, you need to include nine vital components. With these nine in place, you will get results:

- Powerful headline
- Basic story of your company (very brief)
- Proposition
- Exact offer
- Guarantee
- Call to action
- Your name
- Your location
- Your Unique Selling Position (USP)

- **Create a Unique Selling Position.** Your Unique Selling Position (USP) tells potential customers what you have that the competition doesn't. Do you sell a unique food item? Does your decor have a particular theme? Those are the types of things you can use for your USP. Whether you put it in writing or not, you need to at least mentally have a USP in order to differentiate yourself from your competitors. Remember, a restaurant that doesn't stand out, won't be around for long.

- **Avoid cliche-filled marketing copy.** The worst thing you can do is fill your sales or marketing copy with overused descriptions, such as "mouth-watering" or "it melts in your mouth." Instead, try to describe your product by using your five senses. How does it smell? What do you see when it is served? Make a list of all the words you'd use to describe an entrée, then combine those into an original description. The same idea works for a description of your restaurant.

- **Follow the AIDA principle.** The AIDA principle will help keep your sales materials on track and persuasive. AIDA is simply a four-step process. By using these four steps, you create a letter, brochure, Web site or postcard that will get the results you want.

105

- **Attention:** Start out by grabbing the readers' attention (with a great headline, a powerful claim, surprising statistics, etc.)

- **Interest:** Next, develop their interest (explain your unique positioning statement)

- **Desire:** Make them desire your restaurant (offer enticing descriptions of your food and service)

- **Action:** Finally, call them to action (urge them to visit today)

- **Write your own copy that sells.** Sometimes a limited budget means you have to handle the copy writing for your sales campaigns. Don't worry. You don't have to be Hemingway or Shakespeare to create effective sales copy. Just keep these tips in mind: use "you," keep it simple, appeal to emotion, be direct, be positive, be honest, keep sentences short, repeat your restaurant's name and use testimonials. If you use these tips in your own writing, you'll see results even without the help of an expert.

- **Keep all writing active, concise and simple.** All sales writing needs to meet these three guidelines. You want your message to be grasped quickly and easily by the average customer. It also needs to be concise; use as few words as possible to get your meaning across. Write your copy, then go back and remove every word that does not have to be there. You'll probably be able to eliminate 10-20 percent of the content. Thirdly, your writing needs to be active. An example of an active sentence would be: "Restaurant X provides great service." On the other hand, a passive sentence would be: "The service at Restaurant X is great." Active writing needs to be full of powerful verbs like provides, gives and delivers, while avoiding linking verbs (e.g., is, are, was, etc.).

- **Develop a sales kit.** A sales kit can come in handy when you are trying to land the "big fish." Let's say you want to sell nearby businesses on holding their business lunches at your establishment, you would send or personally deliver your sales kit to the head of the company. A professional sales kit includes an information sheet (details about your products/ possibly a copy of the menu), testimonials, business cards and a map. You can also include a voucher for a free lunch so that the decision-maker will have a chance to try you out before making that final decision.

- **Create a catalog.** You may not think of a catalog as effective sales material for a restaurant, but it can be. Just like a retail catalog, yours would include pictures and descriptions as well as prices. These catalogs could be sent out to businesses and organizations with which you hope to do business. Not only will your catalog be imaginative and unique, but it will also do a better job of enticing hungry potential customers to stop by. Another advantage: your catalog can be created using a scanner or digital camera for pictures and your office computer software.

- **Create informative literature.** You're probably wondering what type of information you could offer customers other than your menu. But the fact is you have a lot. You can write some copy about staying healthy with low-fat, low-sodium foods (using your menu for examples). You could write about certain cooking techniques, discuss the history of favorite ingredients or give creative cooking tips. You can distribute this info as part of your restaurant's newsletter, pass them out at schools and organizations or leave them on your tables for customers to read.

- **Learn the art of headlines.** Have you ever seen copy written for those get-rich-quick schemes? They are highly effective at attracting sales. Their headlines are part of the reason. Your sales and ad copy should always have a headline. However, not just any headline will work. People are most interested in headlines that promote how products will benefit them, announce something new and offer practical advice. Statistics, questions and surprising facts also work very well.

Create a Mailing List

Developing a mailing list and database is really an essential part of marketing. The good thing is that it costs you next to nothing, especially if you already have a computer with database or spreadsheet capabilities. The real challenge is determining how to collect the information for your list (this is where the contests, business card drawings and customer satisfaction surveys come into play). For the most part, you can build a fairly large database of names and addresses just from these activities. At the same time, you'll be successfully marketing. Some POS systems can also collect this information for you. Involve your waitstaff, give them a small fee for each completed database card. When creating a mailing list, bear in mind the following factors:

- **What information to collect.** The essential part of your mailing list database is:

  - Name
  - Address
  - Zip code
  - Spouse's name
  - Telephone
  - E-mail address
  - Fax
  - A line that allows permission to fax and e-mail the customer
  - A line, perhaps, for likes and dislikes, favorite foods, etc.
  - Critical information (e.g., birthdays and anniversaries and a question about private functions they may hold each year)

- **Develop a direct mail campaign.** A direct mail campaign will require two things: a mailing list and a good mailing piece (letter, brochure or postcard). You may want to consider doing direct mail campaigns with a very particular focus; businesses, families, lunch crowd, etc. When you do a campaign like this, make sure to divide it up into smaller sections. If you plan to send coupons or discounts with the letters, put a different code on the coupons for all sets so you can track the results.

- **Remember the five Ps of direct mail copy.** Essentially, you want to give potential customers an idea of what they can expect with a photo or with descriptive writing. You also want to make them a promise (to deliver lunch within 30 minutes, to provide great food at good prices, etc.). Use testimonials or facts to support your promise and encourage them to take action (come in today and find out for yourself, call now to make reservations, etc.). Finally, add a P.S. at the end, possibly with your phone number or a discount offer.

- **Here are the five Ps of direct mail copy:**
  - Picture
  - Promise
  - Prove
  - Push
  - Postscript

- **The importance of the zip code.** With the zip code information, you can accurately determine from where your business is coming. Chances are you'll find two or three zip codes are delivering the majority of your customers, so when you distribute flyers, rent mailing lists or volunteer for community activities, make sure you focus on those areas.

- **Include irresistible "bait" with mailing.** If you think of sales as fishing, you know you need good bait in order to lure in your customers. Offer a free sample, a free drink or a contest entry that can only be checked by bringing it to the restaurant. These types of bait generally do the trick.

- **Send lottery tickets with mailings.** Here's another possible form of bait: scratch-off lottery tickets. Include one in each mailing along with a letter that wishes them luck and invites them to spend their winnings on a fabulous dinner at your establishment. The winners will be grateful enough to come by and the non-winners may be so impressed with your generosity that they come in as well. Losing tickets can be redeemed for $1 off so everyone wins.

Extra Tips for External Marketing

Here are a few more essential tips and possibilities for marketing your restaurant:

- **Avoid marketing based on low prices.**
  Consumers typically don't mind paying more for great food, excellent service and a pleasant atmosphere. When it comes to buying a tube of toothpaste or bottle of soda, however, it's a different story. Avoid using cheap prices as a selling tool; it won't bring you the customers you need for success and will hurt your bottom line in the long run.

- **Use repetitive marketing.** Some salespeople are of the mind that your materials need to be unique each time. If you think of the most popular ads and sales gimmicks, the reason they worked was because of the repetition of a particular theme, character or line. You need to do the same thing once you find a sales piece that delivers results. When the time comes to change campaigns, decide which elements of the first one to keep and build around it.

- **Send gift baskets to potential clients.** If you're trying to land a luncheon, special event or a strategic alliance, consider sending a gift basket. The basket should include samples of some of your best food, plus a letter expressing your desire to work with them (using the AIDA principle). Make sure to include a business card so they'll have your name and contact information. Deliver the basket personally and then follow up with a phone call in a couple of days.

- **Conduct a telephone marketing blitz.** This tactic will work best directed toward businesses. Hire a local telemarketing firm or use your staff to call selected businesses in your area. Ask if they've heard of you and if they've ever dined with you. If the answer is yes, get their feedback about the experience, then offer to fax them a menu, a list of specials or some kind of discount. If they haven't, go into your spiel about the food and the restaurant, then invite them to come in. Give them someone to ask for and provide them with exceptional service. Afterward, give them a bounce back certificate to encourage them to return.

- **Market to local teams and organizations.** Sports teams, nonprofit groups and clubs in your area are a great place to target some of your marketing activities. After games and meetings, these individuals are going to want a place to eat, relax and talk. You need to be that place. Start off with one organization. Send them a polite letter of intro- duction, a brochure and discount coupons. In the letter, you may want to tell them that you have private meeting rooms available by reservation or that you welcome large groups so they'll consider bringing the entire meeting to you.

- **Sell benefits.** One of the mistakes inexperienced salespeople tend to make is to focus on features, not benefits. You can talk about the high-quality steak, the fresh-picked strawberries or the rich cream sauce of your food until you turn blue in the face, but customers just won't be convinced. Those are simply features, no different than telling a customer his new CD player holds 100 CDs. His response: So what? The idea is to show the customer why those features can benefit him or her. With the CD player example, the salesperson might say it would allow him to listen to hours of continuous music, house his entire collection and impress his friends. With your food, you want to stress how the high-quality steak will melt in their mouth, the strawberries will make them swoon with sweet delight and provide a romantic and sensuous dining experience. "Sell the Sizzle – Not the Steak."

- **Market to college students.** One of the most overlooked groups of diners, unless you're talking about pizza delivery, are college students. Generally, they lead hectic lives with working, studying and socializing, so most of them rarely cook for themselves. Consider sending out brochures or coupons to college campuses. You could host a college night with entertainment and special prices or offer students a discount when they show their school ID.

- **Ask everyone how they heard of you.** If you want to track your sales and advertising effective-ness, you must find out how your customers are hearing about you. Many restaurants rely on those customer-satisfaction surveys to get this type of information, but not many people actually fill those out. Either you or your manager should circle the dining area at least once an hour asking guests how their experience is going and posing the all-important question: How did you hear of us?

Publicity

Do something mediaworthy. The best way to get publicity (often free!) for your restaurant is simply to do something newsworthy. You might sponsor a local team, donate food or money to a charity, take part in a fund-raiser, visit schools to speak to students, etc. Don't just take part to get the media attention; do something you really want to do. The effort will seem more sincere and will be better received by your potential customers. Here are some great possibilities:

- **Broadcast your success.** If you're doing well, don't keep it to yourself. Send out press releases to let potential customers and your competition know you are doing great and plan on being around for awhile. The idea is that people like to do business with people and places that are successful. After all, if other people like you, then maybe they will too.

- **Write/distribute press releases.** Any time your restaurant or staff does anything newsworthy; winning a contest, saving someone's life, creating a new recipe, etc., you should write a press release announcing it to the media. Since you're distributing locally only, the costs will be minimal.

- **Develop a press kit.** You've probably heard of press kits in connection with big events or movie releases, but you never thought you'd ever use one. Now is the time! You can develop your press kit to send to local newspapers, television stations and magazines in order to entice their journalists to pay your restaurant a visit or to cover a special event you are hosting. Most press kits are not difficult to put together, but they should include the following items: letter of introduction, summary sheet (lists all contents of the kit), your biography, a press release, photographs, fact sheet (provides information about your product) and advertising materials.

- **Include a profile of your patrons in your newsletter.** While it may not get publicity for you, it will for your customers. If you send out a newsletter regularly, include at least one profile of a customer in each issue. The profile might include their first name, occupation, favorite food on your menu, favorite beverage and any other info they want to provide. Choose regular customers for the profiles and post the newsletter openly in your restaurant (perhaps even leave a copy at every table).

- **Join your local chamber of commerce.** One of the easiest ways to spread the word about your company, especially with other businesses, is to join the local chamber of commerce. As an active member, you'll get to meet other business leaders and will have an opportunity to network with people who may very well help you increase your sales. In fact, you could consider holding meetings at your establishment.

- **Window posters.** Draw in a lot of attention; make your restaurant or your message stand out in a big way. Consider window posters or large signs and banners around your restaurant. Let people know about your specials or upcoming events, but don't overdo it.

- **Airplane.** Think about hiring an airplane to fly over local events with a banner advertising your restaurant or dropping coupons out of the sky.

- **The ever-popular balloon.** Place an advertising balloon in your parking lot or anchor it at events and large gatherings to gain big exposure. You'll definitely become a topic of conversation!

- **Have local celebrities make appearances.** Most people in the area are interested in local celebrities. Maybe your high school's marching band could drop by for a little performance or the mayor could come by to shake hands with his constituents. The possibilities are endless. To find potential "celebrities," keep your eye on the news and your ear open for names people talk about frequently. Also, don't forget to consider the reporters on local news broadcasts or radio station anchors; they usually attract quite a following.

- **Sponsor parade floats.** Most towns have parades at least once a year, sometimes more. But you can't have a parade without floats and each float needs a sponsor. Think of the crowd that your local parades draw, then think of each of those spectators watching a beautiful float bearing your restaurant's name as you go by. Put little children on the float dressed like chefs and servers or put members of your actual staff up there to smile and wave. Or, donate the float to a worthy cause that would love to participate but cannot afford to make their own. You may even get more recognition because of your selfless act.

Holiday Festivities and Special Occasions

People enjoy celebrating the holidays and no celebration is complete without delicious food. Make the most of each holiday by creating special promotions that will make hungry diners bring their celebrations to you. Here are a few suggestions (in chronological order) for traditional holidays as well as a number of unusual special occasions that will give your restaurant an excuse to throw a party.

New Year's Day

- **Serve traditional "good luck" food.** Did you ever hear the tradition of eating corned beef and other foods on New Year's Day to ensure that you'll have a great year? Consider offering these items on your January 1st menu.

- **Start a New Year's resolution contest.** For the first week of January, invite your guests to write down their resolutions for the coming year. Hold onto the lists, then in two to six months give them a call and check on their progress. Invite the successful customers in for a special celebration.

St. Valentine's Day

- **"How We Met" contest.** Do your customers come in dreamy eyed and blissful? They may be the perfect candidates for a "How We Met" essay contest. Start the contest in early January and invite couples to write a brief essay, 500 words or less, detailing the romantic tale of their first meeting. Select four to five of the winning entries and invite the couples to your restaurant during Valentine's week for a free romantic meal. Include the winning essays on your Web site, in your newsletter or post them in the restaurant. Make sure to also send a certificate for a free dessert or bottle of wine to every entrant.

- **Romantic dinner packages.** When you plan a romantic evening, you want everything to be in place. Your restaurant can make things easier by offering complete packages. For one price, include any or all of the following: dozen roses, limo ride, bottle of champagne or candlelight dinner. You may even want to take the promotion one step further and partner with a local hotel so that romantic diners feeling amorous after the meal can continue their perfect evening until morning.

Engagement Night

You can work this promotion in two ways:

- **The first way is to host an engagement night for couples getting ready to tie the knot.** You can take reservations and offer private, secluded dinner areas. Also, make sure to include a consultation with the groom-to-be so you can help him plan the perfect way to pop the question.

- **The second way is to hold a party for all of the past couples who became engaged at your restaurant.** In both cases, make sure to include lots of champagne, romantic mood music, candles and a menu full of aphrodisiacs.

- **Singles' night.** Sadly, Valentine's Day is not a happy event for all people. Invite those individuals to a special evening of mingling, dancing and fun. You may want to call it an anti-Valentine's Day party. Not only will your party help ease the sadness of the day, it may also help singles form a love connection.

Presidents' Day

- **Cherry festival.** So maybe George Washington didn't really cut down a cherry tree, but that doesn't mean you can't use some juicy cherries to celebrate his birthday. Consider adding a cherry pie to your menu or using cherries to garnish all of your drinks. Find unusual cherry recipes and add them to your menu for the whole month.

- **Penny sale.** In honor of Abraham Lincoln, you can give customers a reason to use all of those pennies that weigh down their pockets and purses by having a penny sale. The typical approach is to offer entrées or drinks at full price, then the second only costs a penny. An alternative is to say with any ticket over $20 (or upwards), patrons can get a dessert or an appetizer for only a penny.

St. Patrick's Day

- **Green beer.** This classic March 17th beverage still brings in the customers. Even though the only real difference is the food coloring, people love to try something different. In fact, you could offer other drinks with a more leafy shade: milkshakes, sodas or water, so those who don't care for beer can also get in on the fun.

- **Leprechauns.** While normally torturing your serving staff is not a good idea, you can make an exception on this day and ask them to dress up like leprechauns. The guests will find it amusing and some of the servers will enjoy an opportunity to get out of those regular uniforms for a change!

- **Pot o' gold contest.** With leprechauns and four-leaf clovers dotting your establishment, it seems like a good time to hold a contest. The variations are endless with this one and you can even drag it on through the entire month of March. Customers have to find a rainbow in order to win. You can place the rainbows on cups, napkins, game tickets, under tables, even on the bill. If you want to prolong the game, make the customer find pieces of the rainbow.

April Fools' Day

- **April Fools' fun.** With this type of celebration, you'll be giving your servers a chance to be creative and have fun. Allow them to try to trick customers by telling them outlandish things: the soup of the day is tarantula gumbo. Need extra breadsticks? No problem, I'll just add the $25 to your bill.

Easter

- **Easter egg hunts.** Children love Easter egg hunts. Consider holding a special hunt just for them. You can either use your restaurant's dining area (if you are closed for diners), your parking lot, or a different location that you've selected. Make sure that the prizes the children can win include free food from your restaurant.

- **Easter Bunny photos.** Parents love photo opportunities with their children and children love the Easter Bunny, so rent a costume and bring him in. You may even want to hold a special lunch or breakfast reservation-only meal with the bunny.

- **Easter basket meals.** While grown-ups might not go for it, consider serving all of the kids' meals in Easter baskets instead of in the usual fashion. The baskets should be reusable and should contain small pieces of candy and maybe a plastic egg or two. Consider stocking up on eggs and baskets during after-Easter discount sales.

Cinco de Mayo

- **Mexican fun.** In recent years, this Mexican holiday has grown in popularity in the United States and more restaurants are throwing parties. For your festivities, add some entrées with a Mexican flavor, if you don't have some already. Offer specials on tequila and Corona, invite a Mariachi band to perform and bring in some piñatas.

Mothers' Day

- **Mothers' Day essay contest.** This essay contest is a wonderful one for children. They can write a short essay on why their mother is important to them (topics can vary). You may want to pick several winners in different age categories. Then, pick the best essays and invite the authors and their respective mothers for a free lunch during the week of Mothers' Day. Make sure to send a copy of the essay along with a certificate for a free dessert or appetizer to the mothers of the non-winners.

- **Offer free meals.** Mothers' Day is typically one of the busiest for restaurants, but that doesn't mean competition for those appreciated mothers of the world isn't fierce. Stand out by offering free dinners for all mothers. The family will come to your restaurant and while they still have to pay for themselves, the matriarchs' meal will be on the house.

- **Mothers-to-be special night.** Women who are expecting may not consider themselves mothers yet, but that doesn't mean you can't hold a wonderful celebration for them. Provide them with a free meal (or dessert/appetizer), nonalcoholic champagne and a pleasant atmosphere. It'll be a night they'll remember. Have special signs made up for the parking spaces "Reserved For Expectant Mothers."

Memorial Day

- **Free flags.** Show your restaurant's patriotic side by passing out free flags to all of your customers. They'll appreciate the sentiment behind the offer. An alternative would be to distribute coupons for a free flag cleaning at a nearby dry cleaner.

- **Picnic food.** People love a good Memorial Day picnic, but because of weather or lack of time, many simply can't host their own, so do it for them. Instead of your usual fare, offer traditional picnic foods (possibly a buffet), such as fried chicken, baked beans, coleslaw, etc. Cover the tables with red and white checkered tablecloths or open up your outdoor dining area. You also won't want to forget the traditional picnic beverages, such as lemonade and iced tea.

Fathers' Day

- **Fathers' Day essay contest.** Just like mothers, fathers need to know that they're special. Right after your Mothers' Day contest closes, open one up for essays on dads. Again, open this only to children. Pick winners and invite them in for a special meal on the house.

- **Father-and-child night out.** In most families, the children don't spend much time alone with their dads, so this Fathers' Day, hold a dinner only for those two groups. Not only will it give children a chance to bond with their dads, it will give dad a chance to unwind and relax with their children.

Fourth of July

- **Fireworks.** If your restaurant isn't near your town's fireworks spectacular, then you can make your own or invite your guests to bring theirs. Make sure to clear out your parking lot and to clear the event with any businesses in the surrounding areas. Pass out sparklers and pop-its to children, then put on a small display with fountains and low-danger fireworks. Avoid using bottle rocks or other types of fireworks that leave the ground unless you hire a professional. Not only are these dangerous to you, but they increase the risk of injuring a spectator or damaging property.

- **Red, white and blue.** Since the Fourth of July is a celebration of patriotism, why not redecorate in red, white and blue? Create some interesting and colorful menu items, such as Patriotic Nachos (blue tortilla chips, red salsa and white sour cream). The only limit is your chef's creativity.

Labor Day

- **Celebrate the workers**. The first thing you should do on Labor Day is to thank all of your employees and reward them in some way for their service. Secondly, make the day an opportunity to show appreciation for all the other workers in the world. You may want to offer discounts to people of working age or give them a free beer. You could also hold a drawing for a vacation; the perfect prize for any hard-working folks.

Veterans' Day

- **Celebrate the veterans.** For one day only, offer all veterans a free meal to show your appreciation for their service to their country. Chances are they'll bring their families along, so you'll still get some paying customers as well.

Oktoberfest

- **German celebration.** Just as with the Mexican Cinco de Mayo, this German festival is the perfect excuse for you to have some fun. Add some traditional German food to your menu: bratwurst, sauerkraut and beer are the big three. Invite a German band to play some polka music and have a great time.

Halloween

- **Trick or treat.** Many parents feel nervous about taking their children door to door anymore for Halloween, so give them an alternative. Prepare small treat bags including a coupon for a free kids' meal and pass them out at your door to guests and trick or treaters alike.

- **Costume party.** People love to dress up for Halloween, so give them a good excuse to do so. Invite them in for the party. Serve Happy Hour foods and alcohol. Hold a costume contest. You may even want to include traditional Halloween party games, such as bobbing for apples. Keep in mind that this party should be for adults only.

- **Food platters.** If they don't want to come to your party, at least they can give you some of their money. Create platters of your best appetizers or snack-size portions of your best entrées that can be sold for other parties. Take orders for the platters in advance so you can make sure to be prepared.

- **Coupon books.** Because many parents don't like to give their children a great deal of candy, you can get in on this by creating coupon books and selling them to customers throughout October. The coupons should be for items a child would be interested in: free kids' meals, free desserts, etc.

Thanksgiving

- **Meal platters.** Not everyone has the time or the ability to make a scrumptious Thanksgiving dinner for their families. Save them the trouble by selling ready-made platters of food. Although traditional food goes over best, you can be a little creative with side dishes. Make sure to include desserts as well. Take orders ahead of time only.

- **Thanksgiving Eve specials.** For those men and women who slave away all Thanksgiving Day to prepare a home-cooked feast, they deserve a chance to relax before the cooking begins. Offer discounts or specials on the Wednesday before Thanksgiving, but make sure they don't fill up on turkey and cranberries before the big day!

Christmas

- **Santa Claus.** Don't hesitate to bring jolly old St. Nick into your restaurant to attract the children and for photo opportunities. Make sure he brings plenty of candy canes and a Polaroid.

- **Choir performance.** Nothing sets the Christmas mood more than a choir performing holiday songs. Invite local school or church choirs to sing for your customers throughout the month of December.

- **Pre-wrapped gift certificates**. You probably already know that gift certificates are a great way for your restaurant to get into the holiday shopping spirit, but you can increase sales by going that extra mile for your customer and providing them pre-wrapped. Also, consider setting up gift certificate kiosks in local malls and shopping centers in December to make it more convenient for customers to pick your certificate as the perfect gift for every hard-to-buy-for family member.

- **Shoppers' special.** Christmas shopping is exhausting, but it also works up your appetite! If you're located anywhere near a major shopping area, you could offer a discount to people who come in and show a receipt from any of the surrounding stores. Ask those stores to promote the savings as well. Another alternative is to reward shoppers with food dollars for every $10/$20/$30 they spend in the nearby shops. With the food dollars, they can either purchase their meals or gift certificates.

New Year's Eve

- **Early Bird special.** Most New Year's Eve parties don't start until late in the evening. Offer a dinner special to those getting a jump on their festivities. You may want to accept reservations and pass out party favors or balloons. Make sure to keep everything upbeat and fun so that your guests get their party off to a good start.

- **Package deals.** If you decide to offer a New Year's Eve dinner package, make sure that it is a reservations-only experience. Serve an early dinner. Make sure to have plenty of entertainment on hand and keep the cash bar open. Have party favors available and make sure the restaurant is decorated with streamers, balloons and banners. Include at least one glass of champagne with each package. Another possibility is to partner with a nearby hotel to include an optional hotel room in the package. But most importantly, do not allow any of your intoxicated guests to drive. Arrange for a taxi to be available throughout the evening for those not able to drive. Also, offer a discount on the package for designated drivers.

Other Unusual Occasions

The following unusual occasions may provide you with yet more marketing opportunities. Consider the following:

- **National Soup Month (January).** Broaden your soup menu to include some unusual new recipes or different takes on classics, such as chicken noodle. At the end of the month, ask customers to vote on which new soup(s) should end up on the menu.

- **Chinese New Year (February).** Add some Asian touches to your restaurant this month. Pass out chopsticks and give fortune cookies with each meal. Include more traditional Chinese dishes on your menu. Make sure to add some beautiful golden dragons to your decor.

- **Chocolate Chip Cookie Week (March 5-11).** Let your chef go wild with cookies during this week. Design a variety of chocolate chip cookie variations to sell to your customers. Or, have a chocolate chip cookie bake-off with customers as contestants and your chef as the judge.

- **National Pecan Month (April).** Pecans don't just have to be a topping. Add this delicious nut to some of your existing recipes, including salads. Try to use them in creative ways or simply replace your bar's peanut stash with the nut of the month.

- **National Hamburger Month (May).** So you're not a fast food restaurant, that doesn't mean you can't celebrate National Hamburger Month. Create brand-new patty creations, such as stuffed burgers, peppercorn burgers, Mexican burgers or veggie burgers.

- **National Barbecue Month (May).** If your restaurant already focuses on barbecue, then this is the time for a big party. If not, try adding a few traditional tastes to the menu. You can also hold a barbecue sauce cook-off with patrons as contestants or with chefs from nearby restaurants competing.

- **National Dairy Month (June).** Sour cream, ice cream and butter on everything! You may want to make that scoop of ice cream free this month. Other than that, try to emphasize the dairy aspects of your most popular recipes. This might also be a good month to introduce a specialty butter for your fresh bread.

- **National Blueberries Month (July).** These sweet blue treats can be used in so many ways. Add blueberry bagels to your breakfast menu, create some new blueberry desserts, drop blueberries into drinks as a garnish, add bowls of them to your buffet, etc.

- **Peach Month (August).** A sweet peach is pure heaven in the sultry days of August. Does your menu have Peach Melba? Now's the time to add it. Do you serve peach-flavored ice tea? Put it on the menu. You might even want to create a peach sauce to flavor one of your best pork dishes.

- **Mustard Day (August 3rd).** Celebrate during Happy Hour by offering discounts on drinks and providing Happy Hour foods that taste great with mustard, then offer a variety of mustard varieties:

honey, brown, spicy and yellow. Don't forget to make those dishes that require mustard or mustard seed as an ingredient a feature or special this August 3rd.

- **Chicken Month (September).** If you'd like to expand your chicken offerings, this would be an ideal excuse to try out some new recipes. As people move away from consuming so much red meat, more and more are flocking to chicken as a replacement. Try a variety of dishes using chicken prepared in a plethora of ways: fried, baked, broiled, steamed, etc. Then let the customers pick the best for the menu.

- **Honey Month (September).** Draw attention to the most overlooked sweetener of our time. Drizzle it over desserts, add some to your teas, cook chicken in it or simply leave it on the tables for customers to use as they see fit.

- **National Pasta Month (October).** Bring out the spaghetti, fettuccine and manicotti and celebrate in October! If you don't already serve a lot of pasta, add a few to your menu. Pick traditional favorites, such as ravioli, but don't shy away from coming up with something original. For example, if your restaurant focuses on Mexican food, make a salsa spaghetti.

- **World Vegetarian Day (October 1st).** Shock your patrons by serving no meat whatsoever on this day. Create some fabulous vegetarian entrées and invite guests in for a taste test so they can learn for themselves that food can still be wonderful even without the meat.

- **Homemade Bread Day (November 17th).** Nothing smells better than freshly baked bread, so fill your restaurant with the breathtaking aroma. For one day, make a variety of fresh breads for your customers to enjoy and make sure to include your special butter spread or honey as a topper.

Miscellaneous (But Marvelous) Marketing Tips!

There are always a few tips for restaurant success that don't fit into any other category, but you'll find them here. Unlike the other tips in this manual, these may cost more to implement. However, in the long run, they will help you develop multiple streams of income for your restaurant. You may wish to explore the following possibilities:

- **Add a store, bookshop, etc.** Many restaurants have included a small shopping area where they sell their own merchandise or other items that fit into the theme of the establishment. For example, Cracker Barrel's restaurants have a shop modeled after an old-fashioned country store. As people wait for their seats or stand in line at the cashier, they can browse through the candy, shirts, toys and knick-knacks. What you sell depends on the audience to which you're marketing.

- **Develop merchandise.** Along with the store, you may want to consider developing some merchandise to sell at your restaurant. T-shirts, baseball caps and coffee mugs with your logo all make great gifts and souvenirs. Alternatively, you could brand a line of cookware, or package some of your special sauces, seasonings or even entrées and sell them under your restaurant's name.

Again, visit sites such as www.myron.com, www.ahrpromtions.com or www.tagdesigns.com to see what is available. However, if you have an idea that isn't listed, don't hesitate to inquire if they can work with your idea. Many designers welcome a challenge.

- **Produce a cookbook.** As a restaurant, you are most well known for your cuisine. If you produce a cookbook including some of your best recipes, it is sure to go over well. The cookbook will not only bring in more income for you, but it will also spread the word about your restaurant. Plus, if people read through your recipes, they may pay you a visit just to taste your fabulous creations for themselves.

- **Plan to attract banquets and parties.** A great way to increase business is to actively pursue big events, such as special-event banquets and large parties. Simply create a brochure and a sales letter that outline the type of food you offer, the nature of your site's atmosphere and the quality of your service. You may also want to send them a sample basket or a sales kit. Begin advertising that you handle banquets and large parties so people will begin to see you in this new way. Make sure, however, that you have the room to handle these big groups without disturbing your regular patrons.

- **Start a catering service.** Catering requires a little more work than hosting a banquet. For one, you need a mobile staff and transportation. You also need to develop a catering menu, which may or may not differ slightly from your traditional menu. One of the most popular catering events are weddings, so be prepared to spend some time with brides-to-be in order to help them select a menu for their reception. Make sure to outline a pricing structure that is profitable, but competitive.

- **Choose unusual décor.** Nothing is worse than going into a restaurant and looking around and thinking that you've been there before even though it's your first time. Your decor needs to make your establishment stand out. It needs to make a statement about you, your food and your staff. Be unusual. Check out your competition, see what they've done, then do the exact opposite.

- **Use an exhibition kitchen.** One of the reasons sushi bars are so popular is that people get to watch their food being prepared by a terrific chef right before their eyes. It's entertainment and eating rolled into one. You may not want to serve sushi at your restaurant, but you can still have an exhibition kitchen. A plexiglass window would do the trick. The challenge is that your kitchen must be in top shape at all times. One slip up and the entire restaurant is aware of it. But if you truly want to be unique, an exhibition kitchen is the way to go.

- **Develop a discussion group.** If you're thinking about making major changes to your marketing strategy or to your restaurant, you may want to start a discussion group. Include yourself, several top staff members (including servers) and a few regular customers. Talk about changes, do taste testing and brainstorming ideas together. With the group, you'll be able to get feedback right away from all of the people who will be affected by your changes and you won't have to worry about making a horrible mistake.

- **Survey customers about food, service, etc.** One of the most important things to keep in mind is that it's the customers that matter. If you make a change, you want to make sure the customers are happy about it. Consider conducting regular customer surveys. You can conduct surveys over the phone or create survey forms for them to complete. Ask them about the food, service, atmosphere, etc. Most importantly, reward them for their time and listen to their feedback. Some of the most valuable suggestions you'll ever receive will come from your customers.

Future Success

The marketing and advertising strategies and suggestions contained in this manual can dramatically increase sales and customers at your restaurant. Remember that these are guides, so use them to trigger your imagination. Add your creative flair and don't be afraid to take a calculated risk now and then. Just make sure you do the research and the planning first. Here, finally, are a few pointers for the future success of your thriving restaurant:

- **Make sure you have the room and staff for an increase.** Before you implement any of the ideas in this book, make sure that you have the staff and space to accommodate an increase in business. Many restaurant owners believe that adding more customers is the only way to increase profits. If you don't have enough resources to handle 20 or 50 more customers a night, but you bring them in anyway, you'll end up with long lines and bad service, which will result in bad publicity for your restaurant.

- **Focus on short- and long-term goals.** The key to marketing success is to think long-term but act short-term. Essentially, you need to decide now where you want your restaurant to be in two years, five years, even a decade and start setting small goals that will help you get there. As you accomplish each small goal, you'll feel better about yourself and your restaurant.

- **Live up to customer expectations.** Nothing is as vital! If you promise your customers high-quality food and fast service, but deliver only average food and slow service, you're not likely to get many repeat customers. The key is not to promise customers more than you really can deliver, so when you exceed their expectations, they are dazzled. Remember, when a customer has a better-than-expected experience, he or she will tell their friends and they'll have higher expectations, so your staff and you need to be constantly improving.

Good luck and happy marketing!

INDEX

M
mailing list, 79, 108
marketing, 11
marketing notebook, 12
mascot, 88
meeting rooms, 21
Memorial Day, 122
menu, 27, 31, 39, 103
menus for holidays, 37
merchandise, 131
monthly promotion, 11
Mother's Day, 121
mug club, 25
music, 15
mystery shoppers, 55

N
names, 34
New Year's Day, 117
New Year's Eve, 127
newsletter, 115
newspaper ads, 93
nonalcoholic, 31, 32
nutritional information, 36

O
Oktoberfest, 124

P
pagers, 14
pasta, 130
patriotism, 123
pets, 17
phone directories, 95
photo, 34

picnic, 122
Polaroid, 71
postcards, 18
posters, 115
President's Day, 119
press kit, 114
press releases, 92, 114
private dining rooms, 72
profits, 11
publicity, 114
punch card, 21

R
radio, 93
radio stations, 80
record cards, 58
refills, 29
refunds, 58
regulars, 23
reservations, 68
restroom, 14

S
salad bar, 40, 53
sales kit, 107
samples, 20, 28, 70
Santa Claus, 126
scheduling, 68
schools, 89
server, 52
service, 67
service mission, 67
side dishes, 28
signature drinks, 31

soft drinks, 31
souvenirs, 73
special occasions, 19, 116
specials, 50
St. Patrick's Day, 119
St. Valentine's Day, 117
staff, 43, 49
staff meeting, 48
story, 32
substitutions, 30
suggestion box, 56
suggestive selling, 10
Sunday brunch, 40
surveys, 55
SWOT, 10

T
table settings, 13
tag line, 95
takeout, 39
target audience, 12
teachers, 89
telephone marketing, 112
television commercials, 93
Thanksgiving, 125
ticket stubs, 62
training, 47

U
uniforms, 50
Unique Selling Position
    (USP), 105

V

valet service, 18
value, 35
vegetarian, 29, 130
Veteran's Day, 124
voucher, 17

W
water, 54
Web site, 86, 101, 103
weekends, 71
wine, 31, 32
word of mouth, 65, 69
writing, 106

Z
zealot club, 22

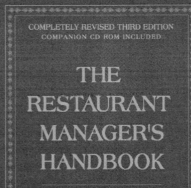

Your #1 Source for Books, Videos, Training Materials, Tools, and Software

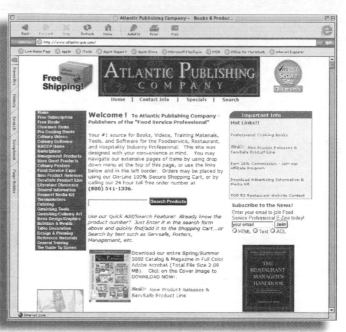

Especially for the Foodservice, Restaurant, and Hospitality Industry Professional!

Our web site was designed with your convenience in mind. The search feature makes it easy to find exactly what you're looking for and there are over 1,000 items to choose from. Orders may be placed by using our online 100% Secure Shopping Cart. Simply the best reference for the food service professional!

www.atlantic-pub.com

If you enjoyed this book, order the entire series!

1-800-541-1336 Call toll-free
24 hours a day, 7 days a week.
Or fax completed form to:
1-352-622-5836 Order online!
Just go to **www.atlantic-pub.com**
for fast, easy, secure ordering.

Qty	Order Code	Book Title	Price	Total
	Item # RMH-02	THE RESTAURANT MANAGER'S HANDBOOK	$79.95	
	Item # FS1-01	Restaurant Site Location	$19.95	
	Item # FS2-01	Buying & Selling A Restaurant Business	$19.95	
	Item # FS3-01	Restaurant Marketing & Advertising	$19.95	
	Item # FS4-01	Restaurant Promotion & Publicity	$19.95	
	Item # FS5-01	Controlling Operating Costs	$19.95	
	Item # FS6-01	Controlling Food Costs	$19.95	
	Item # FS7-01	Controlling Labor Costs	$19.95	
	Item # FS8-01	Controlling Liquor, Wine & Beverage Costs	$19.95	
	Item # FS9-01	Building Restaurant Profits	$19.95	
	Item # FS10-01	Waiter & Waitress Training	$19.95	
	Item # FS11-01	Bar & Beverage Operation	$19.95	
	Item # FS12-01	Successful Catering	$19.95	
	Item # FS13-01	Food Service Menus	$19.95	
	Item # FS14-01	Restaurant Design	$19.95	
	Item # FS15-01	Increasing Restaurant Sales	$19.95	
	Item # FSALL-01	**Entire 15-Book Series**	**$199.95**	

Best Deal! **SAVE 33%**
All 15 books for $199.95

Subtotal	
Shipping & Handling	
Florida 6% Sales Tax	
TOTAL	

SHIP TO:

Name_____ Phone(_____) _____

Company Name_____

Mailing Address _____

City _____ State _____ Zip _____

FAX _____ E-mail _____

❏ My check or money order is enclosed ❏ Please send my order COD ❏ My authorized purchase order is attached
❏ Please charge my: ❏ Mastercard ❏ VISA ❏ American Express ❏ Discover

Card # ▢▢▢▢-▢▢▢▢-▢▢▢▢-▢▢▢▢ Expires ▢▢▢▢

Please make checks payable to: **Atlantic Publishing Company** • 1210 SW 23rd Place • Ocala, FL 34474-7014
USPS Shipping/Handling: add $5.00 first item, and $2.50 each additional or $15.00 for the whole set.
Florida residents PLEASE add the appropriate sales tax for your county.